Are We There Yet?

A Guide to Conquer Every Twist and
Turn on The Journey to Success

Jeffrey Peterson

Are We There Yet? A Guide to Conquer Every Twist and
Turn on The Journey to Success

Published by:

Table of Contents

Introduction

"The man I am chasing is the better version of myself, the man I am capable of becoming, the man I was put on this earth to be." —Ed Mylett[1]

I'm sitting here in my office, having finally wrapped up a long day of work, and I can't seem to get a thought out of my mind. This morning, I was walking Chase, my dog, and saw a young man mowing someone's lawn. I knew it wasn't his home because as I passed him, he was finishing up, and I saw him go up to the front door and collect his paycheque, then go back to the lawnmower to give it a quick clean before moving on to the next house.

With a quick rap on the neighbour's door, the kid was out there again, revving up the lawnmower and weaving his way over the overgrown grass. As I paused there watching him, I thought about whether or not he owned the lawnmower, whether he bought it himself for his business or borrowed it from his father to earn a little pocket money. I wondered how he found his clients and what price he negotiated for himself. Was this enterprising kid saving for anything in particular, or did he just want the freedom to go out to the movies without asking his parents for an extra twenty bucks?

He reminded me of the unlikely journey that led me to where I am today—from my days mowing lawns to now owning

_____

[1] Mylett, Ed. #Max Out Your Life: Strategies for Becoming an Elite Performer. (JETLAUNCH, 2018).

and managing a real estate group and overseeing businesses that run the gamut from construction to consignment.

My venture into business didn't start with a trust fund or any other safety net; rather, it started with a burning desire to defy the odds and create something meaningful for myself and my family out of what little I had. From those early days of uncertainty to the bustling empire of Peterson Properties, LLC, my path has been anything but conventional. You might look at me and think I went straight from high school to college into an executive's chair, but little did you know I spent more time in thankless, grueling jobs learning about business and discovering what I truly wanted from life.

Reflecting on my journey, I realize it wasn't just about the businesses I built or the successes I achieved; it was all about the lessons I learned along the way — lessons I hope will guide you on your path. One of the most significant lessons was the importance of adaptability. I had to learn to pivot quickly when circumstances changed and trust my instincts to take calculated risks to push myself. I had to learn to be resilient and bounce back whenever someone told me "no." These skills were not innate; they were developed through experience and perseverance, and my story will show that no matter your circumstance, you can also develop those skills. It's about the people you meet and how you'll learn from them along the way. It's about being open to new experiences and what those experiences have to teach you about your own life.

Through grit, determination, and more than a few twists of fate, I have managed to forge a career that sustains me and fuels my passion for growth and innovation. I'd like to invite you to join me on a tour of my life and business opportunities, reflecting on the lessons I have learned. It's an unorthodox journey marked by resilience, humour, and the unwavering belief that with enough perseverance, anything is possible. Together, we'll explore my highs and lows, the victories and the setbacks, as we uncover actionable strategies that have propelled me from humble beginnings to a thriving career in real estate.

Looking back on my life, I'm reminded of that young man I saw this morning as he diligently cleaned his lawnmower before moving on to the next house. I see a version of myself in him, driven by curiosity and a desire to better his life for himself and his family. I see that same determination and work ethic I had when I first started, the kind of professionalism that is rare in a teenager. I am reminded that with enough perseverance and a willingness to learn, anyone can achieve their goals, no matter what they are.

In these pages, I want to share my story and the strategies and lessons that have helped me along the way. I hope to inspire others to pursue their passions and never give up on their dreams. I hope to show that anything is possible with the right mindset and a commitment to growth.

CHAPTER 1
Humble Beginnings

"Persistence is to the character of man as carbon is to steel" —Napoleon Hill[2]

The first lesson I learned was perseverance, which would serve me well for the rest of my life. When I was around nine or ten, I went camping with my brother Gary every weekend. We lived in North Carolina, where pine forests and open fields were calling for adventure. Our parents were often busy running their small upholstery business, so Gary and I were left to entertain ourselves -- and we kept each other busy. We didn't do anything crazy, and our parents could always expect us to be home after our adventures, but we still made it out, no matter the weather.

Come rain, sunshine, heat, or even snow (just once), Gary and I spent every single weekend outdoors, and we never waited for the world to happen to us. Instead, we sought how to keep ourselves entertained and busy, often camping out for the weekend. Those camping weekends and the fight against endless boredom instilled a sense of independence that would inform my life for years, teaching me to adapt to new circumstances and think quickly on my feet. Camping taught me to learn from any failures before trying again and again.

On one of these camping trips, Gary and I ran into a troop of Boy Scouts out on their first camp. Of course, we knew of the

---

[2] Hill, Napoleon. *Think and Grow Rich*. Cleveland, OH: The Ralston Society, 1937.

Scouts, but I don't think we had ever considered joining until then. I didn't think I needed the scouts to teach me what I had already learned, and the idea of camping with a group seemed more like a nuisance than any kind of fun. Gary was a little more interested, and he kept trying to convince me that the scouts would be a good time, but I couldn't get past the fact that after two months, I would be promoted to the rank of "Tenderfoot!" Can you believe it? How could I be promoted to a rank that made me seem like I was tiptoeing through the woods to avoid getting a splinter?

Eventually, Gary joined, and I followed because I didn't want to be left out. I'm glad I did; I was in Boy Scouts from the age of thirteen until I aged out at seventeen and became a scoutmaster of my troupe at 21. The program taught me to be independent and persevere, and it taught me valuable leadership skills I would never have learned anywhere else. It taught me that having a goal is the best motivation to move forward in the world.

I quickly rose through the ranks of scouts, becoming an Eagle Scout after only two years and collecting a few palms once I did. As an Eagle Scout, I became a leader within my troupe, a responsibility I took to heart — with a brief detour once I got my driver's licence at sixteen. I was a teenage boy with a driver's licence! I could have abandoned Scouts and left behind the Eagle badge, but I knew I had a responsibility to my troop. Not only that, but not many people achieve the rank of Eagle Scout, and I knew that badge would make me seen as a responsible and distinguished man later in my life, the kind of person who took on an endeavour and saw it through no matter how difficult it was.

My childhood was spent camping every weekend, no matter the weather, and I committed to Boy Scouts right to the very end. It cultivated perseverance and leadership skills that are essential in business and development. Looking back, I see that camping out with Gary every weekend wasn't just a bonding experience between brothers. It set the stage for all the skills I would learn later on in life in a hands-on environment where all those skills would be tested. The ability to stay focused in the face of stormy weather, adapt your strategy, and push through difficulties is crucial for achieving those long-term goals and getting your business to survive and thrive in the wild.

To Lead and Persevere

"Character consists of what you do on the third and fourth tries." —James A. Michener[3]

Perseverance and leadership skills are crucial in the competitive world of real estate, where challenges abound, and success often hinges on navigating disaster. I have always said (and I will say so again) that the definition of good luck is where preparation meets opportunity. To be successful in real estate, it is essential that you persevere and find that opportunity and also have the skills to prepare for it. Early life experiences play a significant role in shaping these qualities in a person, influencing how people respond to obstacles and lead others. When aiming for business success, reflect on your early life experiences, how they might have taught you these important skills, and how those lessons can be used again in real estate.

The Nature of Perseverance

Perseverance is "the persistence in doing something despite difficulty or delay in achieving success." It's about the steadfast, stubborn resolve of doing something, even though it's hard and you might not get it right away. We teach this to children as they learn how to read or tie their shoes and later when they're learning how to drive — or, as in my case, when

---

[3] James A Michener. *Chesapeake, "Rosalind's Revenge"*. New York: Random House, 1978.

they're working on their Scouts merit badges. It enables people to push through challenges, maintain focus, and stay committed to their goals. In the business world, perseverance is essential as professionals frequently encounter setbacks like market fluctuations, client rejections, and complex negotiations.

Early life experiences can significantly influence someone's capacity for perseverance. Factors like family dynamics, educational opportunities, and even socioeconomic conditions can foster or hamper resilience early on. For some, these experiences can encourage risk-taking and problem-solving, while others learn to follow-the-leader and stay in the safe lane. That type of follower thinking can create a fear of failure, leading to a person who rejects potential opportunities that can hinder your business growth — and if you can't chase an opportunity, you won't get very far in the world of real estate.

Unfortunately, we can't change how we grow up, but we can change how we look at things when we are older. Those who faced a lot of criticism or lack of support in their early lives may struggle with perseverance, so it is essential to find a change in mindset to succeed.

Achieving a Growth Mindset

A "growth mindset" is the belief that your abilities, intelligence, and talents can be developed through dedication, effort, and learning. It emphasises that challenges and failures are opportunities for growth rather than obstacles that force you to give up. The real estate business is fickle and littered with obstacles; you will never succeed without a growth mindset. It's essential to remember that when someone tells you "no," that is simply an opportunity for someone else to say "yes." Not all of us had this idea reinforced when we were young, which means we have to learn and reframe our brains as we grow up. Even if you did and have been able to nurture your perseverance, these exercises are good practice for those days when everything seems to go wrong.

#1: Research Famous Failures

You are not alone. When the world closes a door, tons of people are on the same side as you, which hasn't stopped them from succeeding. Reading about a few famous failures can help you understand that you are not alone, that your failure isn't unique or life-ending, and that if you keep trekking through that mud, you might end up at a clearing sooner than you think. J.K Rowling, for example, was a single mother living on government support who faced rejection from twelve publishers before she finally heard a "yes" for her little book, Harry Potter and the Sorcerer's Stone.

#2: 3-2-1 Exercise

The 3-2-1 Exercise teaches you to learn from your failures as you move through them to your next venture. When faced with a setback, ask yourself the following three questions:

- What are three things I have learned?
- What are two things I want to learn?
- What is one question I still have?

These three simple questions help you reflect on setbacks objectively, focusing on growth and learning instead of dwelling on negatives or self-criticism. Even those with a healthy growth mindset can benefit from this activity, as I help you analyse your business decisions and grow from them. A growth mindset means you're focused on developing yourself and your business, which means that even when you succeed, you're thinking about what you can do to take the next step forward. The 3-2-1 questions help focus your efforts so that you are moving forward in a considered way and making steps towards a goal, rather than developing your business like an octopus — with flailing tentacles all over the place.

Goal Setting and Development

Goal setting is a crucial part of business development and something you'll have to get used to to be a successful leader. In the world of real estate, in particular, it's essential to have an idea of where you're going so you aren't wasting time and money on investments that will bleed you dry in the long run. For example, if your goal is to get into commercial real estate, opening your profile with a piece of commercial land rather than a residential one is important. This will prime you for the specific challenges you'll find when dealing with commercial properties.

Once you have some experience, then comes time to expand and diversify, but when starting it is crucial to set specific goals to focus on. Not only that, but setting goals and sticking to them is an important leadership skill, one that will provide direction, clarity, and motivation for yourself and your team. By establishing clear, measurable objectives, you can align your efforts with the business' vision, encourage collaboration and communication, and help your team members understand their roles within your organisation. Ultimately, proper goal setting, combined with a growth mindset, drives performance and fosters an environment of curiosity and continuous improvement.

Leadership: The Partner to Perseverance

You don't have to be a leader to practice your leadership skills. In fact, you'll probably fare better if you don't wait for that opportunity to come knocking. As a kid, I joined Boy Scouts of America, where you practice leadership skills and self-motivation through earning merit badges and mentoring fellow scouts. Without the organisation, I may have become a fantastic camper who could take care of himself very well, but I would not have been very good at leading other boys as they worked on those skills themselves.

Being a good businessman and being a good leader share a lot of the same skill set, yet they are two very different roles. A true leader is constantly teaching others and helping them improve their skills, whether in sales, negotiation, or even staging a showing. Think back to the last great manager you had at your job — what made them trustworthy to you? How did they build a relationship with you, and what did you learn under their tutelage? If you can answer all those questions, you know that person has been working on their leadership skills.

Being a solid leader in business means you can guide teams, manage projects, and build strong relationships with your clients and team. Real estate is not the type of business where you want to be solo camping. Staying informed about market fluctuations, being adept at problem-solving, and maintaining composure in the face of challenges is easier on a team as you'll always have a second opinion. Being a leader means listening just as much as delegating and having the emotional intelligence to know when your way of thinking might not be the best way to go, and your expertise can make way for someone else's.

The intersection of perseverance and leadership is pivotal for success in real estate. Perseverance will equip you with the resilience needed to navigate the inevitable challenges and setbacks that can arise, and forming solid leadership skills will help you navigate the many different relationships you'll have with both clients and coworkers. Early life experiences will significantly shape your capacity for perseverance, influencing how you respond to obstacles and opportunities. By fostering a growth mindset from a young age, you'll learn to transform failures into learning experiences, enhancing your ability to adapt and thrive in business. These skills are foundational; upon them, you'll build the structure of your business through grit and hard work.

CHAPTER 2

Working in Tobacco

"Whether you do the work or you don't, there's
always going to be a price to pay."
—*Bedros Keuilian*

My family moved to Richlands, North Carolina, just as I was about to enter the seventh grade. With one summer standing between me and a new school, I had to find a way to pass the time and get to know a few people. Thankfully, I've never been the type to struggle with figuring out how to fill the hours in a day. I quickly became friends with Steve Smith, who lived just down the road and whose father owned a small tobacco farm. One day, while hanging out on Steve's porch, his father stopped us and asked if I'd like a job for the summer. I immediately said yes because, at that age (and, to be honest, any other), I'd do just about anything for a little extra pocket money; little did I know just how grueling that extra pocket money would be.

Steve's dad said he'd pick me up at six in the morning to 'beat the heat.' I had no idea what that meant, only that it could get up to ninety degrees in the summer and that I was sacrificing my days of lying on the porch with a cold drink for a mysterious farming job. That didn't scare me off; I had woken up even earlier while camping to watch the sunrise and take down camp; how much harder could farming tobacco be?

I waited outside the house, and Mr. Smith showed up in his old beat-up pickup truck with about eight other kids, all wearing raincoats. That part confused me — didn't Mr. Smith say we were trying to 'beat the heat'? I'd checked the weather report the night before, and it said it would go up to 90° that day. A raincoat was apt to make someone pass out!

Once we got out to the fields, I saw what the raincoats were for. The tobacco leaves were covered in dew, hanging onto the moisture from the night before. I was quickly soaked to the bone in the cool morning air and practically frozen to the harvester. The raincoats were off by noon. Once the leaves were clipped and the sun was high in the sky, I made a mental note to bring my raincoat the next day.

Our days were spent cropping and hanging the tobacco leaves, as well as any other chores around the farm that Mr. Smith could think of; once in a while, we topped and suckered the tobacco, and I remember one incident where there was a torrential downpour, and we had to dig a few ditches to keep the field from flooding. Mr. Smith kept us busy for every minute we were with him, making sure to fill those hours before we went back to our parents at the end of the day with hard fieldwork. Throughout the summer, you could spot the kids working the tobacco fields by the yellow stains on their skin and the tobacco gum perpetually stuck to their hands. We were a whole crew, and it was the easiest way I've ever made friends, bonded by our backbreaking work and the number of bites you had from the tobacco worms crawling along the plants. It was hard work, the kind of work no one wants to get into, but I'll forever be glad I did it.

For one thing, it reminded me how important it was to get an education and work towards a good job to avoid the manual labour of the tobacco fields. It also gave me the strength of character and work ethic to carry me into my business ventures. There was no time to dilly dally on decision-making, and there was no patient boss who patted your head after every mistake. I cut my teeth on my first job and learned firsthand what it meant to work hard. That is the sort of thing you never forget.

The Importance of Hard Work

It can be easy to forget about real, hard work in today's business world. The kind of work that leaves you sweaty and tired at the end of the day but still satisfied by a job well done. I can't blame anyone who hasn't had that kind of experience. As a parent, I don't think I would want any of my kids working on a tobacco farm at thirteen, but I cannot ignore the strong work ethic that doing so gave me. A job like that reminds you what it means to be challenged and how it feels to work through that challenge towards a job well done, but it just can't be replicated in a sterile office job. The value of hard work and a strong work ethic cannot be overstated in the business world. Understanding the significance of hard work and developing a robust work ethic is essential for personal growth, career success, and a lasting business in today's fast-paced market.

Hard work is the backbone of success, essential for building a career or starting a business. It demands dedication, perseverance, and the discipline to do whatever it takes to reach your goals. Hard work isn't just physical effort; it also requires mental and emotional strength to stay focused and push through challenges. It's about overcoming obstacles, growing stronger, and seizing opportunities—whether it's closing that next deal or forging valuable connections.

It may sound old-fashioned, but it is true: there is nothing like hard work. A new business needs someone who understands the many facets of hard work: dedication, discipline, and perseverance. These qualities can be learned in many ways —

athletics, for example, teaches you many of the same skills I learned on the tobacco field — but no matter how you do it, you need to learn about hard work for your business to succeed.

This probably makes it all sound depressing and unrewarding, but it's not all bad. The menial jobs we have when we're young help build the positive characteristics that will reward us later in life. Challenging jobs help to build resilience as they often require us to face setbacks and bounce back from them. In challenging jobs or menial work, you learn from a mistake once and never make the same mistake again. After that first morning, for example, I always brought a light rain jacket to protect me from the damp tobacco leaves in the morning and keep the sun off my neck in the afternoon. Once you find a solution, you move forward, collecting the reward of what you've learned — this is called resilience. Resilience is the art of adapting and moving on, a vital quality in an industry where there's always someone waiting for you to throw in the towel so they can capitalize on your mistake.

Enhancing Your Skill Set

The true value of hard work comes in enhancing and expanding your skill set. Effort and perseverance can lead to developing new skills and refining existing ones, and continuous improvement is a massive part of building your success in the business world. Working hard involves consistent practice, problem-solving, and learning from experience — elements I briefly described, but we'll go into more detail now. Problem-solving is something you'll see come up over and over and over again — why is that? Well, running a business at a certain point is just solving a series of problems until you think you're finished (when you've started at the beginning again). If you're investing in a new property, you must first solve the problem of negotiating the deal, financing the investment, renovating, and so on. While these individual markers are cause for celebration, at their core, they are a series of problems for you, the business owner, to solve.

So, what does that have to do with hard work? Continuously going back to improve and solve a problem you thought was finished is hard work. When working manual labour or any other physical job, you tackle a series of physical problems. In that scenario, you have no recourse to give up or say no, and you'll just get fired! Working a job like that forces you to revisit a problem repeatedly, and as you do, you begin to practice the skills necessary for solving the problem.

For example, say you have a job working on a construction site. You're tackling various daily tasks, whether demolition, framing, installing drywall, or moving heavy equipment from one place to another! It's hard work; day after day, you are going back to the site, and you have to be ready for whatever the foreman throws at you. That is training your adaptability since you have to be prepared to change your focus at a moment's notice. Let's say you're on the drywall team, and at the beginning of this contract, you didn't have much experience with drywall installation.

Every day you go back, you get faster and more efficient at installing drywall as you learn what works and what doesn't. By the end of the week, you can throw up a wall in half the time you could when you started. You've learned problem-solving skills by analysing what techniques were more (or less) efficient for installing the drywall; you've practiced perseverance by continuing to go back to the same task over and over again; and using deliberate practice, you've applied your problem solving and perseverance to get better at the new skills you learned. Try doing that from behind a computer desk.

Work Ethic and Business

You are probably reading this and rolling your eyes, wondering why I will even bother talking about work ethic. Of course, it's vital to business, and it should be obvious why it matters in real estate, yet I find time and time again that the idea of a strong work ethic and the practice of it just don't seem to align with some people. Work ethic and good leadership have one glaring overlap with a haircut: if it's good, you don't notice it; if it's bad, it's all you can see.

A good work ethic includes a strong grasp of reliability, responsibility, integrity, and commitment. All of these qualities are essential for building trust with employees and clients, and they're all qualities you learn and hone through hard work. Now, I can't go back into your past and change anything, and until someone invents a time machine, you cannot do that, but you can practice that same work ethic in your personal life to bring those qualities into your professional life.

We are all busy people, and your life is about to get much busier because the only way to train back that solid work ethic is to create a responsibility for yourself outside of work. Whether through a class at the local community college or joining a casual sports league, you will get out of the office and head to a place where a group of people are waiting. This is the only way to learn how to put up drywall without switching careers entirely into one where you put up drywall all day. Joining a sports league or a class where you learn a new skill will remind you to be responsible to a team and not give up when learning something new. Not only that, but with this new venture, you'll begin to learn another skill that can't be surgically removed from a strong work ethic: time management. You're already balancing a lot on your plate, and managing your time effectively is the only way to handle it well.

I'm sure you're about to put down this book and move on to another self-help guru who will say all you need is a goal-setter mindset and a dream, but that is unrealistic in real estate. Someone else has worked a crummy job or two, and the memory of it is still fresh in their mind. That person will head to every meeting on time, treat every client with respect, and learn from every encounter how to set up for the next one. At the end of the day, that person will be holding the contract because they've built upon the skills learned from a challenge that is out of their control.

Perhaps you're coming from a different direction, and your memory of that challenging job is all too fresh. While you may want to forget about it and move on to greener pastures, I recommend you don't. The experience of a job where you are challenged every day is invaluable when setting up your own business, as nothing else will teach you discipline like going to a job you hate every day. Your work is just as legitimate as any other, shaping you into the business person you will become.

Not only that, but working for a person you dislike can teach you how to be a better boss in the future! Learning experiences are not always positive; sometimes, you must learn how to turn a challenge into an opportunity for yourself. To cultivate a strong work ethic, you also need to take time to reflect and learn from your experiences. Successes and failures have something to teach us; learning from a bad boss is its masterclass of professional development.

CHAPTER 3
The Bus Driver Chronicles

"Patience is bitter, but its fruit is sweet."
—Aristotle[4]

I got my driver's licence the second I could. On the day of my 16th birthday, the fire of freedom burning inside, I took the driver's test and walked out of the DMV feeling like the world was open to me for the first time. Sure, I had spent weekends in the woods with my brother, and I worked outside in a tobacco field for long enough that I was very familiar with the wind at my back, but nothing could match the feeling of getting that licence. But what was I going to do with it? I was sixteen, I didn't have my car, but I wanted to impress the girls at my high school somehow — I needed some pocket money. I needed a job.

In my time, high school students were paid to drive the younger kids to school. Many people got their driver's licence, then got their bus driver's licence, but few could secure their bus. I was lucky. My sister, Aimee, was a year older and had a bus she was sick of driving. When I got my bus licence, Aimee let me "substitute" for her, and I was driving my bus! It was the perfect job; I had to get to school anyway, so I might as well make money doing it.

On top of that, I got to skip the first half of first period and leave class early to make it to the elementary and middle

---

[4] Commonly attributed to Aristotle's *Nicomachean Ethics*

school on time. The job taught me discipline and how to gain control of a crowd, but I didn't realise it until many years later. I was in charge of 75 kids packed into my bus every morning and afternoon. They were usually rowdy and wired from their day at school, and it was hard to keep them under control. I would often pull over to the side of the road and do homework, waiting patiently until the kids calmed down before setting off again. Sometimes, when they were rowdy, I would fasten my seatbelt, drop the gear super low, and feather the gas — the bus would buck like a wild horse and throw the kids and their books around!

Eventually, the students I drove threatened a mutiny. Their leader, a girl named Margaret, threatened to go to the principal and tell him everything I was doing and how terrible it all was. Now, this little girl was the most trouble on that bus. She often ignored me when I told them to settle down and stood in the aisles—all sorts of trouble that could make riding the bus unsafe.

One day, we had all had enough. The kids were rowdier than ever, and their principal was eyeing my bus in the drop-off line. I stopped the bus and brought their leader, Margaret, to see the principal and settle this matter. Only one of us could win; either the principal would fire me for my creative discipline techniques, or Margaret would find out that I was in charge, whether she liked it or not.

As she was led off the bus, Margaret taunted me with the threat of firing — and I believed her! I wasn't sure how the principal would react, and I was only sixteen! Some of my tactics for controlling them were immature, but I didn't know better then. Back then, they didn't train you to deal with bored and restless elementary and middle schoolers.

The principal met us in the parking lot. He asked me what was going on, and I told him, as clearly as I could with as much confidence I could muster, that the kids were misbehaving on the bus, and I was doing all I could to keep them under control, and that Margaret here was the ringleader. I explained that she'd been standing on the bus, getting quite loud, making it difficult to drive them safely to and from school.

The principal slowly turned his head to look down at Margaret and asked her if it was true. Suddenly, Margaret's bravado faded, and she started kicking at the ground with her feet. She could only say I was always playing with the brakes and wasn't looking where I was going. It came out so meekly from her that I was shocked — I had a hard time believing this was the same girl starting parties in the back of my bus! The principal took one look at me and laughed, told me to keep my eyes on the road, and let him know if I had any more trouble.

Before I tell you this next part, I have to remind you that it was the 1970s, and the rules worked a little differently back then, but still, I was shocked when the principal immediately took out his paddle and spanked Margaret! How was I to know that this would come down on her? I half carried her back to the bus and met the other kids, who immediately scrambled back to their seats.

I could tell they wanted to know what happened, why I was the one coming back with his head held high and not a triumphant Margaret. She sobbed to the others that she had told the principal everything, and he still beat her! Somehow, this proved to the kids that I was in charge, and I never had any problems after that. It was a long two years of driving, but I never gave up, even when I thought the kids would drive me up the wall!

Hard Lessons and Tough Situations

That job might have been one of the hardest I'd ever had, and I am sure that while reading it, you thought of the most difficult and demanding job you've ever had, which mine pales in comparison to. We've all that one boss who drives us up the wall with their strange demands or co-workers who seem to be working against you rather than alongside you.

As discussed in the previous chapter, these difficult jobs are blessings in disguise. They test our work ethic and train us to be better, more efficient workers. You'll almost always work for a demanding client in business, especially real estate.

It's not their fault; your client is looking for their dream home or location, whether commercial or residential real estate. They have a long list of demands for a reason, and it's your job to listen and respond but also remain firm when those demands get out of hand.

No situation will ever be the same, and they will rarely be easy, so it is essential to learn how to handle complicated situations with creativity, patience, and a firm hand.

Patience is a Virtue

At the risk of sounding like your grandmother, patience is a virtue. There may come a time when it is the saving grace between you and a poor decision. Patience is fundamental in business, serving as a cornerstone for long-term success and sustainable growth. In an ever-evolving marketplace like real estate, the ability to wait for the right opportunities, nurture relationships, and allow ideas to mature can lead to more thoughtful decision-making and better outcomes.

Patience allows you to withstand challenges and setbacks and also helps you adapt to new situations. It's often overlooked as a critical component of creative problem-solving, maybe because it's seen as a weak or defensive quality in the headstrong business world. Yet, precisely, this virtue allows leaders to step back, assess situations thoroughly, and devise innovative solutions.

Patience gives ideas a little extra time to germinate and mature into good ideas. Resist the urge for quick fixes over long-term resolutions. You'll find that quick fixes are cheap solutions that require expensive resolutions. The best way to avoid them is to train your patience and stop taking the easiest, cheapest, or fastest path out of a problem.

There's a saying often used in meditation — not a world I'm overly familiar with, but one that frequently offers excellent advice. The saying is: *"The only way out is through."* I've always understood that to mean there's no way around a problem that solves it faster; the best thing you can do is work through it.

Cultivating patience, especially as a business leader, will foster an environment where people are encouraged to find creative solutions to their problems, leading to more effective and sustainable outcomes. Ultimately, fostering patience boils down to one thing: zooming out to see the bigger picture. When searching for a solution to a problem, ask yourself how that solution will help you five or ten years down the road.

If you're deciding whether or not to invest in a property, look around at the neighbourhood and the city you're in and investigate what the property will look like down the line. What is its place in the neighbourhood, and what will you be contributing with this investment? The bigger picture will often illuminate a solution to smaller challenges.

Getting Creative

Decision-making often involves navigating complex challenges and uncertainties. Creativity can play a huge role in this process by providing the tools necessary to explore innovative solutions and make informed decisions. By fostering creativity in your business, you can enhance your team's problem-solving capabilities, helping them adapt to changing environments and maintain that competitive edge that is so crucial in real estate.

One of the significant benefits of getting creative with your business is its ability to help you and your team break free from conventional thinking. We'll see this later on as we delve into the nitty gritty of business development and how to diversify your investments and business portfolio. Still, it's essential to understand why creativity is fundamental to this thinking. Creativity encourages thinking beyond the status-quo and will help you explore new pathways and consider alternative perspectives. This openness to experimentation can lead to novel solutions that might not have been apparent through the bog-standard way of doing business.

So, how do you practice creativity and decision-making? One great exercise is mind mapping and free association. Mind mapping is a visual brainstorming technique that involves creating a diagram to represent ideas, concepts, or information around a central theme. Using branches to connect related thoughts enables you to organise your ideas and explore relationships between them, enhancing creative thinking and leveraging visual cues to spark new ideas.

You start by writing your problem in the middle of a page and then writing concepts and ideas that connect through a web back to that central idea. Not all of the solutions you come up with will be good ones — in fact, a lot of them should be bad — the point of the exercise is to see the connections you can make between these different, seemingly unrelated ideas and solutions to help you expand your mind and get creative.

Mind mapping is an exercise you can implement when a problem requires an innovative solution or want to help expand your mind. The act of drawing connections is what's important here — if you can practise doing it on a page, you'll soon be able to make these seemingly unrelated connections in your mind, and it will help you see seemingly unrelated potential in spaces that others might have passed over.

The Trio of Success — Responsibility, Leadership, Adaptability

Patience is merely a virtue; there's a whole other triad of elements that lead to true success in business. I started with patience because, as we have learned, it takes patience to deal with challenging situations, and without that skill, you won't get far at all, regardless of whether you have the rest. In the ever-evolving business landscape, three key elements stand out as pillars of success: responsibility, leadership, and adaptability. These interconnected skills form the backbone of effective business practices and sustainable growth in any industry. Mastering this triad isn't just beneficial but essential if you want to navigate the complicated waters of today's business world.

Responsibility in business extends far beyond being responsible for your actions. As a leader, you are responsible for yourself and your decisions' impact on your organisation and its people. For example, if you decide to take on an expensive and time-consuming project, you must consider the ramifications down the chain of command.

Are you asking your team to take on more than they can manage? What else are they working on, and what will happen when they shift their duties to include a new project? Are you sinking money into an investment that will get lost at the expense of other projects (or vice-versa)?

Social responsibility isn't optional anymore; gone are the days when our leaders worked in a vacuum and, frankly, good riddance to them! Success has always been a balancing act, and it's always been a team sport. You are the bus driver, and while you are at the head of the bus making sure everyone is safe and getting home on time, you're also responsible for ensuring everyone can behave and perform to the best of their ability so they don't jeopardise the bus ride.

CHAPTER 4

The Upholstery Shop Dilemna

"Communication works for those who work at it."
—John Powell[5]

If I told you driving that bus wasn't my only job, would you believe me? All the while I was wrangling those kids, I was also wrangling furniture and fabric in my parent's upholstery shop. It was easy to juggle the two — I had to get to school somehow, so I figured I might as well drive a bus and get paid for it — but it was harder to juggle the frustration of working for the struggling upholstery business when I could be going out with friends or working towards my future.

I got wrangled because my parents gradually lost all their upholsterers, and my siblings were busy with their own lives. I was responsible, so I had the shop thrust on my teenage shoulders. I wasn't paid and had to learn the business from scratch alongside my mom.

This was the most stressful period of my entire working life. Knowing that he was burnt out, watching my father allow his business to run him down, and having to put in my all, regardless of that, really got to me. It angered me that I had to stay behind while my friends went to college after senior year to help my parents in a job where I didn't earn any money.

---

[5] John Powell, *Will the Real Me Please Stand Up? So We Can All Get to Know You!* (1985).

I knew my father had potential; he was a fantastic salesman, and I'd seen him at work, but that didn't mean he was a good manager. Managing people is very different from managing sales, and slowly but surely, my parents lost their upholsterers. The bulk of the work soon fell upon my shoulders: I did the majority of the upholstery work while my mom did the minor sewing jobs. She also didn't know how to sew, but she learned alongside me, and together, we did whatever it took to make the business work.

Later, I realised that my job made me want more for my kids. I didn't want them to feel the despair and hopelessness I felt as I spent all my summer days working at the shop before biking to a restaurant job at night, so I had a little money to spend. I didn't want them to be working two full-time jobs before they hit adulthood, and I certainly didn't want them to grow resentful of me for forcing that life upon them. I wanted to do more than be a provider; I wanted to be able to mentor my children in whatever path they choose, even when it differed from my own. At this time, I was never expecting to be a rich man, but I wanted to at least pay to ask a girl out on a date and maybe someday make sure my kid could, too.

During that year between high school and college, the year I watched enviously as my classmates went on to start their lives while I was stuck at the workshop, I began formulating the plan to inform the rest of my life. I didn't wake up one morning and decide to go into the real estate business, but I did learn that I didn't want to be in a business I couldn't devote myself to.

I learned that being an entrepreneur or a business owner meant pouring 100% of yourself into your work. It meant having a multitude of skills that could cover all the different parts of your business — you had to sell, but you also had to manage the people around you; you had to save money wherever you could, but you also had to put the time in to find the ways you could make money. I began to plan for what my life might be like once I was free from the trap that was my dad's upholstery shop, a sensitive subject since if I left, my parents would struggle to run the shop on their own.

As a teenager, I had no choice but to work for my father. As an adult, I had every opportunity to avoid bringing my kids into my business — but ultimately, that time working in the shop shaped me into the businessman I am today. Having to learn the upholstery business with no one to teach me and no one to guide me along the way gave me a hard attitude towards the early working days.

If I could manage two full-time jobs and social life, so could anyone else; a lesson my kids learned the hard way. I was always available as a mentor, but I was also always around as the enforcer — it didn't matter that you were out until 5 am, I still expected you to show up for work at eight. Given this attitude, you would think it would cause a lot of tension between my family and me, but it caused the opposite.

Unlike my parents, I could give specific instructions and boundaries to my kids and stand up as a role model. I listened when needed, gave them a shot when appropriate, and let go when it wouldn't work. This is what I had planned for — a situation where none of my kids was trapped in an upholstery shop on a blistering hot summer's day, missing out on their formative years as they watched me slowly burn out and run myself into the ground.

Family Matters

There's a common old saying about working with family:

"Where there's kin, there's conflict."

It takes a determined personality to bring family into business — conveniently, it's the same determined personality that makes for a successful entrepreneur. Working with family can often lead to difficult situations that strain the delicate balance between personal and professional relationships, but there are also considerable advantages to working alongside your kin.

On the one hand, you have a built-in support system of people who will more than likely share your values and long-term vision for success; on the other, you risk having your familiar relationship become collateral damage during disputes or even build resentment between those you love the most. The key to managing difficult situations with family in business is to recognise that they will come up before you ever bring them into business to manage everyone's expectations proactively.

We'll talk more in-depth about some strategies and benefits of integrating family into business later. In this section, we'll focus on handling families' difficulties in business and the importance of planning and personal growth for maintaining these delicate relationships.

The first and most crucial step towards maintaining a successful family/business dynamic is establishing clear personal and professional boundaries. My children poke fun at the way I treated them nowadays, but I know that it is essential for us to have the relationship we have today.

When my kids worked for me, I was their boss. They had the same responsibilities and expectations as the strangers I hired, and I expected them to work just as hard. It may sound harsh, but it was a necessary boundary that I established to instill a sense of professionalism in my children whenever they worked and to avoid the slippery emotional slopes. Implementing professional procedures and politics that apply equally to everyone minimises workplace ambiguity and lowers the potential for conflicts arising from a blurred professional/personal line.

Ultimately, a family business should work like any other — someone is hired to do a job, they are paid for it, and they are assigned tasks and promotions within that business structure. Many family-based conflicts arise from poor communication, in which one misunderstanding snowballs into a major fight that pulls at strings on both sides of your relationship and, therefore, cannot progress reasonably. Creating and maintaining a defined structure for your business, with clearly laid out expectations, is one way to reduce that ambiguity, increase communication channels, and ultimately avoid personal conflicts at work.

This framework also applies to hiring and promotion cycles — you need to ask yourself, why am I hiring this person? Is the reason I'm hiring my relative out of convenience or desperation, or do I believe this is a job they can do well? Do they possess the qualities that will help them succeed in this position, or am I hiring them because I think it will make my life easier or more profitable to do so? The worst thing you could do for your business and relationships is to hire someone who cannot do the work; it will only cause frustration and resentment on both sides. Not everyone will rise to the occasion or use it as a learning opportunity.

In my experience, being dragged into the family business before I was ready led to resentment and aggravation, feelings I had to get over if I wanted to have the same father-son relationship before I started working for my dad's failing business. It is better to do your due diligence and analyse business needs, weighing that against the family member's abilities and goals, integrating them to set them up for success, and encouraging them as they develop new skills.

The opposite also applies: You need to prepare your business to invite clear communication and encourage success so that your family members understand what they are getting into and the stress of learning doesn't impact your personal relationships. This will look different depending on your industry.

In real estate, this may mean explaining to them what the responsibilities of a property manager are and laying out how hands-on you expect them to be. Creating casual or mentorship opportunities before hiring them can help your family become familiar with what you do daily. It will generally give them a leg up in the wider working world.

Jobs like property maintenance teach both work ethic and help demonstrate that running a business isn't all about sitting behind a plaque that says "CEO"; these menial jobs introduce your family to the unseen details of maintaining a property or real estate business. These smaller responsibilities also allow you to observe their strengths outside the home, whether in problem-solving, innovation, or communication.

To maintain a pleasant environment that keeps you from killing each other over the dinner table, it is essential to remember that everyone is different and will bring their own set of skills to the table. You have as much agency as they do in keeping the peace, and the best way to do that is to observe your family and learn their strengths to leverage them in your business. You can also help yourself by setting firm boundaries and sticking to them — no cutting slack because they are your child or spouse. As an entrepreneur, you need to have strong communication skills for positive negotiation and growth, and this is especially true when trying to balance family with business, where you will find your professional patience tested by those who know you best.

As we'll learn later, integrating family into your business can be lucrative and fun. It can enhance your business and make it grow in ways you never would have imagined — but to avoid conflict, you have to meet your family members halfway. You can't force them into a box, leading to resentment in all parts. Instead, it is best to listen, observe, and communicate so you can continue working peacefully at the office and home.

Growth and Communication

Part of the reason to communicate openly with family is to maintain peace in your personal and professional lives. Another is that this open communication can lead to growth potential for both sides, and keeping it open can help you create a growth plan for yourself and your business.

As an entrepreneur, your business can only grow as much as you want; that's why you must plan your growth and stick to it as much as possible. Personal growth shapes your business strategy and leadership capabilities, and it means more than learning new skills or taking classes to improve your business sense; in this instance, the personal growth I'm talking about is more internal — learning from yourself and your experiences to develop your leadership skills, build resilience and adaptability, improve your communication and interpersonal skills, and learn how to embrace change. Once again, there's no class that's going to teach this. Personal growth comes from learning how to listen and respond to the world around you and adapt to make that world work for your business.

Planning for personal growth is difficult, as it differs from person to person. At the end of the day, you are trying to plan how to self-improve, which means taking a long, hard look at your faults and figuring out how to change them. Self-reflection is a skill you will find seeping into every aspect of your business.

- Have you ever done market analysis on a business decision?

- Have you ever had to weigh the pros and cons of an investment?
- Have you ever felt the need to fire someone working for you?

Whether or not you realise it, these skills are flexed when you practice self-reflection. It is the ability to reflect on your behaviours, thoughts, and motivations and how to give yourself feedback to correct them. It takes these skills that you use daily in your business pursuits and puts them in front of a mirror — but why is that important to personal growth, and what does that have to do with running a business?

As you develop a better understanding of yourself, you'll also become more adept at recognising and managing team dynamics and empathizing with customers and stakeholders. Also, personal growth and that pesky growth mindset we keep talking about enable you to bounce back from failures and adapt to new situations with greater ease.

In today's rapidly changing business landscape, the ability to be resilient and adaptable is increasingly valuable, both to protect yourself and your business's interests. As you develop a better understanding of yourself — and, by extension, your business — you will become more adept at recognising and managing team dynamics and your customers and stakeholders. Better emotional intelligence will enhance your ability to build a strong team and communicate openly within your organisation. Soon, you'll see that it will lead to more confidence and strategic thinking, empowering you to take calculated risks and pursue your goals with greater determination.

To truly harness the power of personal growth, you need to approach it with intention by creating a structured plan for yourself and finding a way to stick to it. It doesn't matter where you are at when you decide to get started; the point is to sit down and make a plan — while it is possible to develop slowly and keep a consistent eye on your progress, when it comes to planning personal growth for yourself and your business, it's better to keep to a plan so you can keep track of your progress more tangibly.

You should start with an assessment of your personal versus your business needs. This helps you identify areas of your business that need improvement and helps you set clear and achievable goals in those areas. It also enables you to see where you might get in your way. If some of your personal needs conflict with the business, this is a moment where you can ask yourself if you are working efficiently or if you are sacrificing too much (or too little) when it comes to your entrepreneurial pursuits.

At this moment, it could help to do a SWOT analysis — a breakdown of your strengths, weaknesses, opportunities, and threats — if you are having trouble identifying some of those needs. No business is perfect; yours is no different. A SWOT analysis can identify the gaps in your business that need work and where you might be able to take your hands off the wheel. With a clear picture of where you stand,

Once you have a clear picture of your business and where you'd like to be, the next step is to break down your goals into actionable steps. These actionable steps can be anything, from attending at least three networking events per month to committing to search for new investment opportunities once per week or even walking a different neighbourhood to familiarise yourself with new properties and markets. What is important is to adhere to three universal rules for creating actionable goals:

1. Keep it Simple. Each step should be easy to remember, easy to execute, and clear about what you want to achieve.
2. Keep it Balanced. Each step should not overwhelm or bore you. It should be challenging but not so hard that it becomes unachievable.
3. Keep it Relative — each step must directly relate to the goal you are trying to achieve.

Breaking a goal into actionable steps helps you stay accountable as you work towards your goal and prevents you from burning out along the way. It also makes that goal approachable because you won't be banging your head against the wall trying to figure out how to pull your goal out from thin air; instead, you can work on each of these smaller steps toward the bigger picture. In your entrepreneurial life, you'll sometimes find you need to step back and see the forest from the trees; however, sometimes, you have to look at each and every tree as you make your way out of the forest.

No one wants to be left behind or stuck in a position that doesn't give them the freedom to grow and improve, but at the end of the day, personal growth is exactly one thing — personal. It can only come from within and can only be achieved through self-reflection and discipline. Once you can put a growth plan into place, you can begin to move towards active development and new entrepreneurial adventures, one that helps you unlock the potential of your business.

CHAPTER 5
The College Hustle

"No steam or gas drives anything until it is confined. No life ever grows great until it is focused, dedicated, disciplined." —Harry Emerson Fosdick[6]

Finally, after a frustrating year working for my parents, I enrolled at East Carolina University. I was a year late, but I could still fulfill my college dreams of going out, meeting new people, and taking a leap forward into my new life. I promised my parents that I would come home on the weekends, as their only upholsterer, it was the least I could do, but I told them I had to start on my path, not realising that the path I was talking about was going to be just as hard as the one I was running away from.

I could talk about my time at ECU in two ways: what I learned in school or *at* school. I think the second is more valuable. I studied at school but learned some hard lessons outside the lecture halls. I worked several jobs to pay for school, rent, and gas money; my parents still expected me home every weekend but were unable to pay me.

The second I got to school, I hit the ground running and applied to every job I could find. I finally found a job working as a dishwasher at the local Bonanza Steakhouse. It was not the most glamorous position, but I soon found joy working there. It was methodical work, so I could turn off my brain

---

[6] Source unknown.

for a few hours after class and find simplicity in the routine: collect the dirty dishes from the bussers, wash, dry, shine, repeat.

The only problem was that I got bored very easily in those days. I was too hyper to enjoy the simplicity of dishwashing for long and soon. I was washing faster than the bussers could clear. Finally, I got sick of waiting and started going onto the dining floor and bussing the dishes myself! It wasn't long before the manager, Mike Patinaude, realised that I could do two jobs at once, and he gradually started scheduling me for more hours over the two slow bussers.

For the two bussers, it was a lesson in what can happen when you're slow on the job; for me, it was a golden opportunity. I pointed out to the manager that I was saving him a lot of money. He was saving the wages of two bussers thanks to my initiative (and hyperactivity), so I made him a deal: I wouldn't ask for a raise as long as he taught me how to cook and provided me with a reference at the end of the school year, referring to my experience as a cook.

I knew there was a Bonanza Steakhouse back in Jacksonville, and I had figured out that the menu between the two restaurants was pretty much identical — thank you, chain restaurants! I didn't want to go home for the summer as a lowly dishwasher, so if I could get Patenaude to train me on the grill, I could apply to the Bonanza in Jacksonville, NC, as a cook -- earning me a lot more money over the summer than if I'd gone back to washing dishes for pennies and upholstering couches for free. Unfortunately for me, the restaurant was always so busy that Patinaude never had time to switch me over to the line, and by the end of the year, I still hadn't had any time on the grill.

I didn't let that technicality stop me; before I left ECU for the summer, I asked Mike Patinaude for a letter of reference that clearly stated that I had been trained as a cook. At first, Mike didn't want to agree, he told me that I didn't know how to cook and he hadn't trained me, so he'd have difficulty writing the letter. I reminded him of our promise and how much money he'd saved over the year by having me do the work of two bussers, and I promised I wouldn't embarrass him. I wouldn't take no for an answer, and eventually, he wrote that letter, and I took it straight to the Bonanza in Jacksonville.

The manager, Mr. Price, was an old friend of my dad's — a retired Marine who ran his steakhouse like a tight ship. The afternoon we met, Mr. Price looked me up and down and asked me straight up — *"Do you really know how to cook?"* I was saved by the other cook, who begged him to hire me and let him have the night off. The poor guy hadn't had a weekend off in months, and his desperation was enough for Mr. Price to hire me. I was getting increasingly nervous as I heard myself tell him I could handle the weekend alone. That's how I ended up completely alone on my first day, facing a dining room full of military servicemen who had just got paid. The cook knew what he was doing; I certainly did not.

I knew the basics — make sure the grill is nice and hot, cook the meat on one side, flip it over, and serve when it's done — but I'd never actually cooked for that many people before. Before I knew it, I was behind, and the server was at the window, reminding me that they had customers wrapped around the building and were starting to complain.

I was 75 tables behind (the restaurant had 25), my grill was covered in steaks, and I had no one to cover my hide but myself. In the corner of the dining room nearest the kitchen, Mr. Price sat comfortably, smoking a cigar, laughing, and shaking his head at my misery. He was perfectly calm as it dawned on me that no one would rescue me. If this ship was going down, I was going down with it.

The weekend was a trial by fire, but by Monday, I was a phenomenal cook, and I had learned one of the most important lessons of my business career: If you really want something, you have to pursue it, but you better be prepared to pay the price!

The rest of my college career wasn't as eventful — I married my first wife while still at ECU, so my priorities shifted from those in my sophomore year. I took on a second job at the Waffle House (of all places), helping out the manager whenever unruly drunks were hanging around.

It was the first time I'd encountered a very poor manager, a guy whose anger issues clouded his judgment of every situation, the perfect way to learn to keep a clear head at work. I also managed to squeeze in a construction job during that time, and between three jobs, a new marriage, and school, it was a tough time.

I knew it wasn't sustainable, and when my wife became pregnant, it was time for me to switch gears. I couldn't stay at three menial jobs that paid poorly. I had to start thinking about a long-term plan because the way I was working wasn't sustainable.

On my 21st birthday, I decided to take a leap and start my first business. I had been hustling for years, working three jobs for other people, and I realised that if I put all that energy into my own business, I might actually be able to enjoy my success someday. I was at a crossroads: on the one hand, I could keep working three jobs and going to college, just barely getting by, or invest in my own experience, go to college, and scrape away a living with the potential of enjoying my success later on.

To me, the solution was clear: I would use my experience as an upholsterer, avoid the pitfalls I watched my parents fall into, and build something for my family. It wasn't easy. I started off the old-fashioned way by going all over town and speaking to different furniture stores and interior design shops, trying to persuade them to give me an opportunity to earn their business.

Needless to say, they all had reservations about trusting a 21-year-old college boy with their expensive fabric. My time was coming down to the wire. Without the Bonanza/Waffle House/construction trifecta, I was running out of cash. I had enough money to pay my electric bill or advertise my business in the local paper. It was a big gamble — I could pay for the ad, but there was no guarantee I'd get any business from it. I could ignore the newspaper and pay my electric bill, but there was no guarantee that I'd find any business to secure another month's worth of cash flow.

My upholstery business was a one-man, one-day show. I lived and worked in a two-bedroom home, and one-bedroom was a dedicated workshop. I didn't have a van at the time, so whenever I got some business, I would rent a van at a daily rate. I'd carry the piece into my "workshop" and stay up all night to finish a piece before delivering it (and the rented van) within 24 hours. That's how I advertised my business — 24-hour turnaround service.

You can imagine how some might be skeptical of that, and they made sure to go over my work with a fine-tooth comb. It didn't matter; I knew what I was doing and did good work. I ran the ad in the local paper, gambling that I'd get business before they turned the lights off. My gamble paid off, and I never needed a client from that day forward.

Going After It

If that was a stressful chapter to read, I can promise it was an even more stressful period to live through. The unglamorous part of business development is the beginning when you have more debt than capital and no guarantee that you'll get a return on your investment. That's when all the patience and hard work we discussed comes into play, along with another very important characteristic: perseverance.

In the fast-paced business world, particularly in real estate, it's easy to get caught up in the allure of quick success stories and overnight millionaires, but the reality is far more challenging. You might see a couple of house-flipping shows on TV and think to yourself, *"That's easy! Anyone can flip a house!"* but you'd be forgetting the hours, days, and weeks of renovation work, the unforeseen repairs that force you to rework or go over your budget, and the panic that sets in when the house doesn't sell as quickly as you thought it would. There's a delicate balance between education, entrepreneurship, and perseverance in the face of financial challenges. None of those house-flipping hosts will tell you that chasing your dreams is an expensive project offering zero guarantees.

The Education-Entrepreneurship Tightrope

These days, the value of education cannot be overstated. If you want a long-lasting career rather than just another menial job, you need to have some educational background — but don't confuse "education" with "college." A college degree is necessary if you want to be a doctor, an engineer, or any other highly technical job that could put someone's life at risk. An education can be found just as easily outside the classroom as it can within. The world of business is vast, and while some think you need to rely on that traditional four-year Bachelor's degree, I believe all that degree shows is that you were committed to showing up to the same place, at the same time and getting a piece of paper that proves it. There are plenty of success stories of those who have traded their formal education for entrepreneurship and reaped the rewards ever since.

There are plenty who traded in that four-year degree for a job that has nothing to do with anything they studied. Many people will find they'll be balancing their entrepreneurial pursuits with something else, whether you planned to do so or not, but what you'd like to balance it with is up to you. If you think you need the structure of a four-year degree — go for it! Who am I to stomp on that dream? You'll spend four years studying the book of business principles and theory and network with plenty of people who share your beliefs. I'm here to remind you that if you want to look beyond that structure, you can still find the same education, credibility, and networking opportunities off campus. I should know I didn't end up graduating from ECU — I got too busy running a business.

If you are looking for other entrepreneurs, you must find them and hope they aren't too busy to talk. One way to reach out is to seek a mentorship — formal or informal, whatever works for you — the goal of mentorship is to have someone available to answer questions or consult when you're in a bind. A good mentor will know when to leave you be and when to dispense much-needed advice, but you might not realize it at the time. Oftentimes, feeling like you're playing second fiddle to someone's business can be frustrating, but it can also be the push you need to start thinking creatively and problem-solving for yourself. In this way, you'll see firsthand what it is like to prioritise a business and how to make opportunities work for you.

Whatever path you take, there's no reason to cast aside your entrepreneurial goals. You might be working some menial job unrelated to your goals or ambitions, working for your parents, or studying at college; most important is setting the groundwork for your entrepreneurial pursuits. Starting a business will teach you real-time problem-solving skills, give you a crash course in adaptability and resilience, and teach you some practical financial, marketing, and management skills. So will working in a kitchen. Whatever job you do, you must learn to perform at 100% without acting as if your tasks are beneath you. Why is that? When starting your own business, most tasks will be "beneath you." Running a business when you don't have much overhead means driving your van, washing your dishes, and cleaning up your mess. To succeed, you must learn to perform those tasks with the same commitment as you would: negotiating a contract or breaking ground on a new project.

Hard Times: Financial Struggles and Failures

Part of the reason I'm drilling this sense of commitment is that there will come a time when your business venture teaches you the hardest lesson: how to fail and learn from your failure. That failure may come in many forms: a financial crisis or facing the closure of your business. Either way, you'll be set back a few paces, and if you want to continue, you will have to put in the legwork to crawl back up. It won't be dignified, and you won't be at an arm's length from challenging work, long hours, and difficult decisions.

Entrepreneurship is not for the faint of heart, nor is it for the squeamish. If you are brave enough to replace learning from an expert with learning for yourself, it could be a lucrative practice, but it will inevitably include moments that test your patience and mettle. You will learn the same business theory as your 4-year college counterparts without all the pop-quizzes and history lessons. Those will be replaced with long hours, insecurity, and a test of your resolve rather than theoretical knowledge. At the beginning of my career, I was running my business out of my front room, balancing my clients with the time left on a van rental. They don't teach you that in school; that is a lesson you learn from the world of hard work.

It's important, if you choose this route, to make sure the financial difficulties don't cripple your resolve before you get anywhere. The need for patience and a strong work ethic will be crucial here, as rather than balancing your education and entrepreneurial ideas with structured classwork, you'll be balancing them with risk and possibly a stressful side gig to help you get off your feet. For this path, prior knowledge in the industry you want to build in will be a huge help — without the experience of working at my parents' upholstery shop, I would not have had the confidence and ability to approach as many furniture and interior design studios to offer my services.

I certainly wouldn't have been able to guarantee quality service with a twenty-four-hour turnaround. The buffer you have with balancing work and education is gone, so you must adapt — what is your practical entrepreneurial idea? What expertise do you possess that no one else can match? How can you leverage that expertise so you don't fall flat on your face (and in the red)?

Once again, we are looking to your adaptability to guide you in the face of potential hardship. Those kids getting a degree will have to balance a dead end, boring, or stressful job that leaves them exhausted at the end of a day and dreading opening a book the next — you don't have time to be that tired unless you're ready to face the consequences of it. You've gone after it — entrepreneurship without the foundation of education — now you have to be prepared to pay the price.

Striking the Balance to Persevere

The ideal approach to entrepreneurship combines both education and practical work. This could mean anything from pursuing an education part-time while running a business or working to seeking a mentor from the business community or finding an apprenticeship that works for you. It's essential to remember that education is constant, and it's not always a formal degree.

The goal of education is more than just getting your name on a diploma; it should be to learn from yourself and others continuously and experience to pour that wisdom back into your business. The fact is, no amount of education can prepare you for a financial struggle. Every entrepreneur faces financial challenges at some point, some more drastic than others, and it's during these times that perseverance becomes your most valuable asset.

The balance between education and perseverance calls back to many of the skills already written about in this book, namely adaptability, hard work, and creativity. Your financial struggles can take many forms, and you might not be able to predict them as well as you thought. It could be a cash flow issue with your business, unexpected market changes, or a strain on your personal life and finances that gets you in that hole; the important part is always how you will get yourself out. Do you have to work harder, maybe sacrifice your personal life in favour of long hours, or do you expand your horizons and start looking for work in a new avenue?

These challenges can be demoralising, and may feel impossible to overcome — trust me, I've been the guy standing alone behind a grill full of steaks with no clue how to cook them — but it's important to remember that every successful entrepreneur that you can think of has faced a similar obstacle. The key skill is balance.

Life is a balancing act akin to spinning plates on narrow poles; it looks easy once you've got it, but you'll drop a lot until you do. In business, leadership, and real estate, you're always straining towards that sense of balance, and once you get there, you'll realise you have to topple everything to grow.

CHAPTER 6
Teaching Upholstery

"The beautiful thing about learning is that no one can take it away from you." —B.B. King[7]

Not long after I started Peterson Upholstery, I was approached by a very unexpected client. The local community college needed someone to teach part-time in their continuing education department. They'd been looking for a reliable upholstery teacher to replace the retiring teacher for some time and wanted to know if I'd be up for the task. In my life and experience, I find that opportunities come at you unexpectedly; if you were to stop and deliberate over each one, you'd miss almost all of them.

When they asked, I was knee-deep in my struggling business, and I knew the extra money from the classes would go a long way. My upholstery business was still in its first year, and my first marriage had resulted in a separation. I had an eight-month-old son and was driving a dilapidated pile of scrap metal with wheels (the person who sold it to me claimed it was a 'car') to visit him. I never once missed our time together, but I didn't want him to grow up seeing his dad struggle. Whenever I wasn't with my son or in the workshop, I was catching up with a different pastime — partying.

Looking back on it now, between all of my responsibilities, it was the least sleep I'd ever gotten in my life, and I probably

---

[7] Source unknown.

had no business tacking on a teaching job, but I knew that a little extra money could make my life run a little smoother. Besides, I wasn't a stranger to juggling multiple jobs and a personal life. I'd been at it since I was a teenager, working at my parents' shop while driving a bus, studying, and still making time to do what teenage boys like. I accepted the teaching job before I could talk myself out of it.

The class ran from 6-9 pm, three nights per week. Students would bring in their furniture, and I would walk them through the process of reupholstering it — fairly simple; I just had to make sure I was teaching and didn't take over when they started doing it wrong. Being a continuing education class, most of my students were a little older and were in the class to get better at upholstery for their own good. Hence, the atmosphere was slightly more casual than I had experienced at ECU.

The college needed someone reliable, who would shop up every night, and who knew more about upholstery than the students taking the class — I fit the bill perfectly. Little did they know I was teaching myself on the side! Occasionally, a student would bring in a project with some sewing I didn't know how to do or had an unfamiliar technique; rather than admit that I didn't know how to fix it, I would send the student back to "correct" a previously completed item as homework. In the meantime, I would teach myself how to do the sewing or master that technique overnight. The next day, I would come into class with a completed example and use it as a teaching moment for the rest of the class, the directions clear from the previous night. They never suspected I was only one step ahead of their lessons!

I only slipped up once. For the most part, I was the picture of maturity and wisdom. Any question they had, I found an answer; any problem that cropped up, I found a solution. At the same time, I was enjoying the fruits of being a young man with a steady job and a growing business. The class was over at nine, leaving plenty of time to go out afterward. One night, still nursing a hangover and exhaustion from the night before, I curled up on a freshly reupholstered sofa and told my students to work on their projects and wake me if they needed anything. Three hours later I woke up from my slumber to one of my students telling me that class was over.

"Did anything happen while I was asleep?" I asked. The student hesitated for a moment before telling me that the Dean of the college had come by to check on the class and saw me practically comatose on the sofa. The Dean told the class they should not, under any circumstances, wake me before leaving the classroom. I panicked all night and through the next day, expecting to be met by the Dean's unsmiling face holding a pink slip when I finally dragged myself back to class.

To my surprise, nothing happened. I continued teaching the class, and years later, I finally learned the truth: by the time I started, the upholstery class had been taught for years by a rotating cast of mediocre teachers. The Dean had heard good things about my teaching style from my students and wanted to stop in and see for himself.

My students covered for me, sharing that I was a good teacher who took their questions seriously no matter what they were, and the Dean was impressed. He didn't care that I was asleep;

he wasn't the type to question my motives or hold one bad incident against me. The Dean was results-oriented; it didn't matter to him how you made the journey; what mattered was that you arrived at the destination. When I finally learned the truth, I found out the Dean loved retelling that story as a glimpse into the successful man I would become. He was the kind of person who was so confident in his work that he could sleep on the job, and not a single person around him would complain.

Teaching made it clear that even if I had been working in the upholstery business for years, there was still a lot I needed to learn before I ever called myself an expert. As time passed, I knew I would need to keep updating my skills and learning about my business to keep up with those behind me, who might not know better but would surpass me if I let myself fall asleep on the job.

Learning to Learn Again (...and Again...and Again)

That teaching job was worth a lot more than a funny story about falling asleep on a piece of scrap furniture. It taught me the importance of self-reliance and continuous education. We touched on this topic before, but now we'll dive a little deeper into the importance of self-education and staying ahead through continuous learning.

In the last chapter, we explored the importance of balancing education with entrepreneurial pursuits, especially at the beginning of one's journey. But what happens to that education once one's business is established?

Do you stop educating yourself once you've passed the hurdle of wondering where your next client comes from?

Absolutely not.

Every industry you look at constantly evolves, with new market trends, regulations, or technologies changing the status quo. A successful entrepreneur understands that to keep pace with these changes, you must continue learning about them and adapting them to your business, or else you'll be left behind. If you continue to educate yourself, you can better understand local and global market trends, allowing you to make informed decisions about your business that will help you grow.

Continuous learning is part of having a growth mindset — one of the fundamental aspects of running your own business. If you don't continue to grow, your business won't either, and you'll find that your business will get lost behind others who took the time to keep up with new market trends, technologies, and techniques that improved their output.

In the real estate industry, market trends are constantly changing as neighbourhoods are developed and expanded, and the economy at large weighs on how people buy and use properties. By educating yourself in these and other aspects of the industry, you'll be able to leverage these trends to benefit your business and maybe even expand your portfolio as you learn more about the industry and the factors that can influence it.

The New School: Modern Self-Education

Traditional education follows old methods of learning: structured environments, predetermined curricula, and timelines determined by someone who went through the process and then went straight back to teach it. While that model of education may be valuable for some, it certainly isn't sufficient to keep up with the pace of business today.

Nowadays, a slow shift away from traditional learning models has begun, leading people away from traditional colleges and into different classrooms, tailoring their learning to their specific needs and interests. The new model of keeping up with your education allows for more flexibility and personalisation, and makes it easier to apply what you're learning directly to your job. For an entrepreneur, this is a perfect storm for advancing your career and growing your business — as long as you remain dedicated to learning.

There's no longer a need to squish learning into a few hours every evening or put your goals on the back burner to attain a new degree.

Thanks to the internet, how we access information has entirely changed in the 21st century. Gone are the days when you had to travel to the local community college and hope the guy teaching the class was an actual expert in his field (and didn't fall asleep on the job); thanks to Massive Open Online Courses (sometimes called MOOCs) that are available from universities and industry leaders, you can learn about new subjects and receive new certifications from the comfort of your own home.

You can also join webinars that focus your learning in a few hours if you feel a long-term course won't serve you. Even podcasts and reading apps offer mini-lessons in the time it takes you to make dinner or commute to your job. Technology has revolutionised how we interact and access information, making it easier to scale up your skills. If you want to, it's possible to have access to education from anywhere, and even without a certificate or a degree, education is still valuable if you apply it directly to your business.

As an entrepreneur, you constantly battle for a competitive edge against your peers. In real estate, for example, changes in technology and environmental regulation offer an opportunity to open up your client base and optimise how you do business. Innovations in virtual reality are changing how properties are marketed and can be viewed by potential investors; using augmented reality when touring a property can help investors visualise their ideas for a space even if it's empty, and using virtual reality to tour a property can save time and opens up the opportunity to show your properties to investors in distant markets. Embracing this technology can give your business an advantage by allowing you to reach out to new clientele while saving time and money.

Environmental regulations are changing markets all over the globe, creating new challenges when constructing or renovating. However, learning about these changes could open up your business to a whole new world of opportunities. There are environmentally conscious buyers who are searching for properties that reflect their needs and values and an entire industry of tradespeople who want to demonstrate their skills and innovations to someone who is ready to invest. These are just a few fundamental examples of how new technologies are affecting the real estate industry, and demonstrate how a few disciplined hours every day dedicated to learning something new might enhance your business and lead you down a new and fruitful path — while your competition is left in the dust.

Self-education is not without its challenges. If you are learning new skills or taking courses outside the traditional education system, you must be highly motivated and disciplined since you won't have the structure from learning in a classroom. There's no one looking over your shoulder and checking for your homework, and there's no one to tell you when you need to set business aside in favour of personal development. Not only that, but you have to be motivated enough to sift through the weeds and find high-quality information in the swamp of "experts" online. It can be daunting initially, but sticking to well-known institutions, like online university courses, or asking for recommendations is a good place to start.

Most professional organisations have their courses — some of them are good, many of them a waste of time — but taking a look through their offerings and comparing them to what you see online is another good way to make sure the course you are signing up for is teaching you relevant skills. Reading reviews of books and podcasts or doing a quick online search can also help you familiarise yourself with your teacher and get a sense of what they offer and whether you will relate to their teaching style. Remember that education isn't always about learning in a classroom (virtual or in-person) and is more about what you will take from it. A mentor figure can also be a great educational resource, and it isn't always the person you would think.

Your mentor might be someone in the business community or an electrician who has built a business by overhauling old electrical systems with new, environmentally-friendly networks — it all depends on your goals. If your goal is to grow your business through new connections, a non-traditional contact in an emerging industry might prove more valuable than an old hat stuck in his ways. Both could be beneficial; either could be a dud. No matter what, you must be the person moving it forward — no one can motivate you better than yourself.

Benefits of Staying Ahead

I've already mentioned a few specific examples of why staying ahead in real estate is beneficial. Still, new technologies and the creep of regulation are only one side of the coin. There are many other benefits to staying ahead that are not directly reflected in the skill set you bring to your business but will help your personal development. Staying educated and current can also lead to more creativity and confidence, and I doubt I have to explain why that is so important as an entrepreneur. When someone meets you, they are also meeting your business for the first time — having personal confidence is a significant reflection of how you are going to meet your work.

As you learn, you will begin to explore new topics and unconventional ideas, and you never know who might grasp one of those ideas and trust your business over someone else's. These unconventional ideas lead to new innovations and solutions that will help you meet business challenges head-on or create solutions you hadn't thought of before.

Think of how many people reject using a smartphone; what could they be missing out on? They would be missing out on reaching a new audience using social media, the speed with which they can contact clients and investors, and even the ways they can take their clients along with them, using a tool they can hold in the palm of their hand. Self-education naturally lends itself to critical thinking skills, as it helps create an elastic mode of thought, the kind of thinking pattern that enables you to bounce back from a setback without the grind of disappointment slowing you down.

How to Stay Ahead, Grow, and Learn

The benefits are clear; we've gone over why it's important and how easy it is to keep learning in this day and age — so how are you going to carve out time to learn in a fast-paced business environment? Implementing an effective strategy for self-education requires planning and discipline since no one will hold your hand as you do the work.

Creating a solid routine is crucial for you to get as much as you can, no matter how you do this extra learning. If you want to expand your horizons by listening to podcasts, you need to carve out a time when you won't be distracted by listening to them.

You could always keep them playing in the car, passively listening as you drive from place to place — but how well would you be paying attention?

Can you create a playlist of every song you heard this morning playing on your car radio?

If you can, then kudos to you, and you should consider paying more attention to the road ahead. In general, it's best to create time in your day where you can listen and reflect and write down the great ideas you're hearing. Self-education and improving your skills require discipline if you want to get the best out of it. It will require you to practice some delicate time management skills to balance your business and personal life with education. The balance is vital for motivation so you don't burn out and lose that drive.

Self-education is a powerful tool for staying ahead in the business world. As we've mentioned, learning is a lifelong activity; it doesn't end the day you start your business. It goes through phases of importance and urgency, but it is always there. Learning empowers personal development and growth, creates valuable critical thinking skills, and can nurture innovation in your entrepreneurial pursuits — and if that isn't enough to persuade you, can I add that it can be fun?

We've focused on finding ways to learn new skills and technologies for your business, but learning can also come in the form of developing new hobbies or activities. These can expand your network and even introduce brand-new skill sets that could enhance your work passively. Those students in my college upholstery course were learning a new skill that they didn't necessarily use at work but gave them problem-solving skills and enhanced their hand-eye coordination.

The focus on detailed work had an almost meditative aspect, teaching them to slow down and think about a problem step by step rather than get buried under its weight. Continuous learning can be as informal or formal as you choose, and in this day and age, you are spoilt for choice!

If you want to take a structured class, there are online resources that have whole certification programs planned out for you; if you prefer to learn more informally, there are books, podcasts, and blogs that can help you connect to new information bit by bit, without having to reorganise your whole day around a class. However you structure it, continuous learning is easy and crucial to growing your business.

CHAPTER 7

The Cary Expansion

"The greatest obstacle to success is not external factors, but rather our own limiting beliefs. Change your mindset, change your life."
—Ed Mylett[8]

In 1985, I made the first big move with my business. I packed up and moved to Cary, North Carolina, running my business out of the basement of a friend's house. This move gave me a little more space and a little more flexibility to start moving beyond the upholstery business — something I had been itching to do for years.

Teaching wasn't right for me; it wasn't my calling. At this point in my life, I was still searching for that lightbulb moment that would illuminate my career path; all I knew for sure was that I wasn't going to flip the switch without growing out of the upholstery business. As I've said before, my heart's passion was never upholstery, but I knew I wanted to be my boss, and I had the skills, so I ran with it. In 1985, I ran with it all the way to Cary and took the first step in expansion by getting into the fabric business.

The basement was great for a while, but I quickly grew out of it and started renting a flex space, and from there, the idea for a fabric business to complement the upholstery was born. Ten years later, after going back and forth with every bank

---

[8] Ed Mylett, *#MAXOUT Your Life. (Vervante, 2018)*

that would (or wouldn't) have me, I purchased a dilapidated warehouse in Cary. The place was barely hiding itself together; there wasn't any parking to be found, no doors, no windows, and even no walls! It defined a blank space, and it became the best example of not quitting in the face of unexpected obstacles.

After moving to Cary, I was determined to expand my business. The upholstery game was going well, but I knew I had the potential to do more, and I had the work ethic to match. Selling fabric and building my upholstery inventory complimented the business that was already doing well but required a lot of capital to get off the ground — selling fabric meant maintaining inventory and equipment to cut and store rolls. This meant a trip to the bank.

When I wanted to start selling fabric, every banker I spoke to told me the same thing: *"We see you as an upholstery business, and we don't want you to get hurt."* Hurt by what, exactly? The lack of an MBA or formal experience leading a company that wasn't my own is most likely. The bank was doing its very traditional job of making sure your credentials on paper match up precisely with the request you are making as well — upholstery did not equal fabric in the eyes of the bank. Therefore, I did not have the required experience.

The same went for that first warehouse: *"You don't know real estate, and we don't want to see you get hurt."* By this time, I ' had enough experience under my belt to know I could take this risk. I had taken more considerable risks before, ones that came at the expense of my sleep schedule, and I was confident

I could take on an expanded project. I could visualise what this next chapter of my entrepreneurial career looked like, and I knew that the bankers sitting behind a desk did not have the creativity to share. Finally, I told the bankers what had been festering during our meetings: *"Don't ever tell me what my business is because you'll be wrong every single time."*

I started the fabric business. It was grossly underfunded initially but has evolved into Peterson Consigning Design, and my two kids, Mike and Ashley, are partners in the business. This was the most challenging part of my entrepreneurial career; hearing *"no"* over and over again might have made someone else crawl back their business, but I was determined to expand and knew it could be a success. It was this experience that taught me to never listen to naysayers.

Most people who give you advice don't have experience in what they're advising — your bankers won't know, your accountant won't know, nor will your buddies or your spouse: the person who knows your business best is YOU. Having a clear vision of what your business will become provides the confidence to cast the commentary aside so you can focus on building your business.

Carpe Diem -- Seize The Day and Expand

Whether you stay in the real estate world or you meander away from it, the ability to recognise and seize opportunities will be the difference between success and stagnation. Acting quickly is a powerful driver for expansion, as hesitation can often mean missing out on prime opportunities in today's fast-paced world. By being willing to jump in at 150%, you can position yourself to capitalise on emerging trends and markets before your competitors do — but what are some strategies for doing so? "

Intuition as Analysis

I will always be the first to say that spending too much time analysing your business and the market around you won't get you very far.

Why?

Well, for one thing, the best opportunities aren't going to wait around for you to decide whether or not you are interested. There will always be someone behind you willing to take that leap, and they will overtake you for better or worse every time.

The confidence to act is one of the most crucial parts of expansion and growth, but to do that, you need to train your intuition and instinct. Intuition — the gut feeling that tells you whether or not you should run into that burning building or let it crumble to the ground — is a valuable tool when evaluating growth potential. While data and analysis have their place, sometimes (oftentimes) the most successful business expansions come from your ability to sniff out an opportunity, listen to that gut feeling, and act quickly.

The tricky thing is that I can't explain how to train your intuition; a honed gut feeling comes from life experience and from making mistakes and learning to recover. You can always make the best-informed decisions with real-world analysis: hit the pavement and start learning about the area.

Where are you located? What else is there around you? What are the signs that show the area is up and coming, and what are those that show they are on the decline? For example, if an area has a trendy new salad bowl spot, you can reasonably determine that there are at least a few offices with young people craving a trendy and healthy fast food place over a sit-down greasy spoon.

This form of analysis is more practical and has the added benefit of helping you get to know the culture, people, and businesses in an area where you'd like to invest. A gut feeling can sometimes be dismissed in favour of extensive data analysis from behind a computer. Still, that gut instinct is backed by practical life experiences (including failures) that can refine your entrepreneurial instincts and help you act faster regarding investment decisions.

As you hone that gut instinct, your business experience will start to seep in as well, giving you the confidence to react quickly when making business decisions, the confidence to say no to opportunities that don't align with your core values or long-term vision, and the acumen to determine how valuable they will be in the long run.

The confidence to act on or step away from an opportunity can help you to make big moves and seize opportunities that might have been lost in a moment of hesitation; it also teaches you when to let go of those that won't serve you, one that might have caused more risk than reward if you pounced on it in a moment of panic. Confidence is a skill; it's essential to know when to turn it on and when to dial it down so you don't end up putting your foot in your mouth.

There are some practical things you can do to help you hone that confidence when it comes to your business and start working on your risk management skills at the same time. These are more data-driven areas of business analysis, but it's the kind of activity you can do once and continue to refer to as you start working on those more intuitive growth areas.

Set Your Success/Failure Benchmarks

Determine what success looks like regarding an investment or real estate opportunity. Success may be a property that is easily developed into residential units or is ready to be flipped. Success and failure are unique; by doing this exercise, you will hone in on what success looks like in your worldview, and you'll be able to immediately filter out the opportunities that won't serve your unique vision of success.

In doing this short exercise, you may also find that your vision of "success" and "failure" is different from what you thought it was before. For example, you might have started your business hoping to develop real estate for residential use. Still, while examining your success/failure benchmarks, you realise that "success" for you also means seeing a revitalised neighbourhood, with a thriving business community.

It's possible that your old idea of success might not be serving your goals anymore; this exercise will help you refocus and reprioritise — maybe you'll set up a map of the part of the city you'd like to focus your efforts on. The benchmark is an external marker to train that internal "gut" feeling. In this case, you'd use it to let go of opportunities that fall outside of that geographic range and won't be fulfilling for you in the long run.

The Benchmark exercise makes it tantalisingly easy to fall into a giant trap — uncreative decision-making. As discussed before, creativity will help your business grow and develop over time and keep you competitive within your market. The benchmark exercise enables you to determine the parameters of success, making it very easy to start ignoring what could happen if you think outside the box. This exercise is helpful to make sure that, while you're developing your business instinct, you don't spread yourself too thin or go completely off track; it's crucial that you don't completely close yourself off to potential opportunities that fall a little outside your benchmarks.

Let's continue with the business community example — let's say an opportunity comes up on the opposite side of town, way out of the geographic boundaries you set up for yourself. The opportunity is for a warehouse, which will require more development but can also house a few different businesses and maybe some studios for a mixed-use space.

The space has the potential to grow — but it is outside your benchmark; does this mean it is a bad opportunity? The benchmark helps you gauge your gut — if your gut is looking at this space and exploding with ideas, it's time to throw the benchmark out the window.

Success and failure are, in some ways, highly subjective. You could have a thriving business in a town you hate — successful because you're making a lot of money, but still a failure if you aren't in the place you'd like to be. Benchmarking and developing your gut instinct are the first steps in growth and expansion, as they help you carve out a path for your business. These strategies are more practical than a typical five- or ten-year plan because they give you more flexibility and freedom to pursue potential out-of-the-box opportunities.

Leveraging Technology for Expansion

Once you have a clear idea of where you want to go and the risks you're willing to take along the way, it is time to start creating opportunities out of the resources around you. Business development begins with instinct but is driven by how you apply it to your development opportunities. A significant resource that can help you is, once again, modern technology.

We've previously discussed how, in real estate development, you can leverage virtual reality technology to improve efficiency and cut costs, but this isn't the only piece of tech you can use as you begin to expand your business. Digital market analysis has replaced the slow analysis of the past; using AI tools or data analytics software can help you assess market trends, property values, and all the elements of business potential much faster than you used to. This can be used to quickly get a glimpse into new markets or identify new opportunities for your business to explore.

Project management is also made easier thanks to tech — imagine a day everyone had a rolodex at their desk and waited days for a contract to be delivered between offices. With project management software, you can contact a customer, generate a contract, and have it signed in the blink of an eye while keeping the interaction recorded and archived in customer management software.

Later, you can use property management software to track maintenance projects and communicate with your tenants and your finances across multiple properties. There were days when I had to make sure my kids showed up at work by driving out there and seeing them with my own two eyes. Nowadays, I can be halfway across the country and still know exactly what is going on with every property I manage.

I don't think that technology can replace traditional human communication. Again, relying too much on technology can hurt your ability to adapt or think creatively and could affect the relationships you have with your clients and colleagues. Technology is an accessible way to find and manage new opportunities and get a glimpse into how they will fit into your portfolio or your benchmarks.

Tech can help expand your business without the slow trappings of the past; it is a strategy to enhance — not replace — expanding your business beyond the physical limitations of your neighbourhood or city. Sending someone a contract via email helps develop contacts in different locations, but ultimately, it doesn't replace having an actual relationship with that person, which is crucial if you want to create new opportunities in places far away from your own.

New Locations, New Opportunities

Real growth, especially with real estate, can't happen without expanding your horizons. Real estate is a finite resource; eventually, you'll run out of room to build, come across people who don't want to sell, or face overdevelopment in a city that doesn't need it. To maintain consistent growth, it's critical to expand your horizons — literally.

Expanding your business portfolio and personal contacts by looking beyond your city before overdevelopment can ensure consistent growth. Finding opportunities in new locations demands a lot of that "gut" thinking and adaptability, which I've been harping on for pages and pages in this book. Strategic partnerships and learning about the culture of a place can go far in helping you decide what is the best strategy to follow when it comes to developing a relationship with a new place.

When you expand beyond your town or city, a learning curve needs to be observed if you want to be successful. Every city, town, country, you name it, has its own culture and needs that cater to said culture. Some places won't accept four salad bowl lunch concepts in the whole town; others will accept four in a single block radius; as you move beyond your home base, you'll start to see the patterns of localisation that define your opportunities and growth potential.

Localisation is a concept borrowed from the translation world, and it's known as the process of adapting and customising a product to meet the needs of a specific market in terms of language, culture, local standards and expectations, and legal requirements. In the beginning, you will be your localisation team — you'll be the one doing market research (whether online or on the ground), developing contacts, and familiarising yourself with the legal parameters of your new place. This activity is only intimidating as a concept; the reality of localisation is meeting with fellow business owners, expanding your team, and making new investments — it's the same circus, but you're dealing with different monkeys.

The move is hard but worth it if you want to succeed with a diverse and dynamic portfolio. It's not about growth for growth's sake but challenging what you know about the meaning of "success." It's about recognising genuine opportunities that align with your values and having the confidence and courage to pursue them swiftly. No matter the industry, entrepreneurship is a calling for the curious; it rewards those who want to try something new; without curiosity, your business will not grow.

CHAPTER 8
Banker Battles

Don't watch the clock; do what it does. Keep going."
—Sam Levenson[9]

I've had to battle with bankers to finance my projects throughout my career. I was raised by working parents, and I treated my business the same way. I worked hard and made some money, but not so much that I could throw it around — every step was an investment and a careful one. When I purchased the warehouse in Cary, I was cautious about using the space in the future. This space used to be a cookie factory that needed massive repairs and was going to start its new life as an upholstery and fabric warehouse.

The building could work because it was so minimal that I could do anything with it — the world was my oyster so long as I could secure the funds to gut and renovate the place. I met with a general contractor who gave me an estimate of $50k to get the job done — demolition, renovation, and maybe adding a window or two, and get the dilapidated warehouse up to snuff and ready to be the site of my next expansion.

The estimate fell perfectly into a feasible budget for the project, so I purchased the building. Ready to start the work, I went back to the contractor for a written estimate and was

---

[9] Source unknown, commonly attributed to Sam Levenson, American humorist and writer

met with an eye-opening figure — 500k, enough zeros added to the original estimate to give me a heart attack!

The ensuing discussion was not pleasant, so I'll let you use your imagination rather than describe it here, but needless to say, I did not hire them. This was one bridge I was happy to burn, and a lesson I carried forward with me was to do your homework and do it right before you sink money into a business deal.

I shopped around with every contractor I could find in Cary, and they all said the same thing: it would cost me $500,000 if I wanted to hire someone to demo this building, but I was tapped out. I needed additional capital, and there was no doubt about it. I could only crawl back to the bank to ask for overhead to continue this project.

Of course, the bank turned me down. I went to every single bank in Cary, my plans for expansion in hand, and one by one, they each told me no. I heard every rejection under the sun, including the classic, *"We're just trying to protect you and your business,"* but I was not ready to quit. I owned the building and had to do something with it, but I needed to improve before doing anything.

The bank wasn't going to loan me the money, which meant only one thing — I was going to have to do this job myself. This wasn't the first time I would be learning on the job; the theme of my life seems to have been getting hired and then learning as quickly as I could so I couldn't get fired from running a grill by myself at the Bonanza Steakhouse, to taking over all of the upholstery work as a teenager in my parent's business.

The cookie warehouse in Cary was nothing but a step up for my skills and resolve. With my fifteen-year-old son, Mike, in tow, I demolished the warehouse by hand, working every evening and weekend.

This demolition wasn't for the faint of heart. For starters, the building had 3" pipes wrapped around its insides, 26 feet up in the air — they all had to be removed and filled with old cooking grease. Mike and I built scaffolding and worked, cutting the pipe in sections and letting the pieces crash to the ground. If I close my eyes, I can still smell the grease that oozed out of the pipes in the heat and covered the floor in a sticky mess — I honestly can't believe we ever got the smell out of the walls.

We worked without proper ventilation or electricity, using generators and temporary lights to illuminate our work. As you got closer to the roof, the temperature soared to over 100 degrees in the summer, and there was 1500 feet worth of pipe to cut down. The work was not for the faint of heart.

To this day, I think my job history prepared me to face this warehouse. I had already survived the blazing sun of the tobacco fields, the heat of a grill, a busload of screaming children, and the stress of an upholsterer's workshop; I should be able to navigate the demolition of a dormant cookie factory with only Mike to help.

By the end, Mike and I cut out the wiring, hauled out debris, cut openings in the side of the building to finally create something that resembled a door, and painted the ceilings and the ductwork and the entire exterior of the building to save about $75k on the renovation work finally. By then, I had done everything I could and knew I needed to hire a contractor to get the work done fast, with the force of an entire team of seasoned sub-contractors.

Once again, I went to the bank, juggling my finances to keep the subcontractors working, but they still said no. It wasn't until I sold part of the property attached to the warehouse that the bank finally said yes. Ultimately, the bank that finally said yes turned me down many times before, but I was unwavering in my quest to finance this building before it became a complete disaster.

I knew the project would work and was confident in my plan and vision for the space. I wasn't going to wait around for someone at the bank to have a change of heart. I knew it would be better for me to prove to the bank that I didn't need them to realise my vision and that I would put in the work to make it a success regardless of their help; even though it took a long time, I'm still convinced that this was the key to finally changing their minds. Since then, I've leveraged this investment time and time again by refinancing the building and have pulled out my equity many times to refocus that money on larger projects.

The warehouse in Cary grew to become the Peterson Center, where my "headquarters" is still located. It's still the location for Peterson Consigning Design, now run by my daughter Ashley, and several other businesses. For all the trouble it was getting the property up and running — long hours spent cutting greasy pipe, being given inaccurate quotes from contractors, and having to stalk my bankers until they trusted me enough to provide me with a loan — it's arguably one of the most successful properties I have today.

At the end of its renovation, I divided the property into units for commercial purposes, rented each to different businesses (including my own), and thus turned an abandoned cookie warehouse into an income-generating mini-development! To this day, I've never paid more into the Peterson Center than I've gotten out of it, and I've used the equity in the building multiple times to aid in other projects. It was my first experience in what would become my career — developing properties that had been passed over into gems for the community.

Preparing for Battle

It is a truth, universally acknowledged, that an entrepreneur in need of financing must eventually face a banker. It is always nerve-wracking to sit in an uncomfortable chair as you watch someone comb over your business and financial details, searching for any glitch that might spell failure. My experience has taught me that, especially in times of financial challenges, it's vital that you believe in your business vision and convey so much confidence that the banker on the other side of the table has no choice but to agree to finance you.

For many years, especially as I transitioned from the world of fabric and upholstery into real estate, I faced people who didn't believe I had the "right" experience to lead a new project. Whether they couldn't understand why I wanted to expand into fabric supply or why I wanted to step into real estate, I repeatedly found myself facing someone who needed to be convinced not only that I wouldn't screw it up but that I even had the acumen to put my business plan into action.

Believe it or not, this struggle empowered me in the early days of my real estate career. Whenever someone told me no, I became more determined to prove that their "no" was a mistake, and in doing so, I learned about myself and how to build a resilient front for any potential investor.

I have three rules that, after years of trials (and a few errors), have become my essential guideposts:

1. Make the deal first, then figure it out.

2. Don't make the deal if you haven't done your homework.
3. Value your relationships.

These three guiding principles have led me down a path of success. They are simple enough that they apply to almost every business situation and can help you stay true to your personal vision and values. It's important to remember that no matter who it is, your banker, friends, family — they will pretty much always put you in a box and tell you who you are; you have to be the one to change their perspective; however, it's possible that this perspective will never change, and you have to learn how to work within it.

With bankers, for instance, they will always picture you the way you were at the start of your relationship. They won't see you grow but will measure your requests against the yardstick you first gave them, which can be a major limiting factor as you grow your business. That may mean you have to change lenders as you grow to keep changing out that yardstick so it matches where you are currently, but there are benefits to these kinds of shifts.

For one, this is an opportunity to cultivate new relationships while maintaining old ones, which can be an opportunity to leverage one loan offer against another, should you need to. Another significant benefit is that when a banker changes banks, his loan committee will often extend more flexibility for the first few loans he writes. Maintaining old connections means you will one day have an old banker knocking down your door as he begins to rebuild his client base and can make offers that once seemed out of the question.

A bank only lends money when they are extremely confident that they will get it back; they are not the ones taking calculated risks here. That means when you enter a bank, you have to be twice as confident as they will ever be — never go in asking for money, and maintain an attitude that you are giving the bank an opportunity to win your business.

Even in the most desperate moment, a confident attitude can convey more stability than a piece of paper, or you're sure to leave empty-handed. It's important to remember your BATNA when going into a negotiation, whether with a bank or another business partner — Best Alternative to a Negotiated Agreement. Your BATNA is your trump card when negotiating; it's the plan of action you can take if you need to reject the deal, and it also defines how much you're willing to compromise.

Regarding the cookie warehouse, my BATNA was that I would complete the work myself if the bank didn't provide me with the funds. A strong BATNA aligns with your business vision and provides a point for you to walk away from negotiations that don't serve you, a technique that can convey confidence to the other party and even provide a space to begin renegotiation. Similarly to your success/failure benchmarks, this is a predetermined element of your business plan that can help you make the right decisions as you expand.

In my experience, the best deals are struck when everyone walks away a little bit unhappy or thinking they could have been a little more aggressive to get their way. It's unlikely that a negotiation will result in a perfectly fair deal for both sides; frankly, it is unwise to take advantage of someone you are trying to do business with. It complicates relationships and can burn bridges unnecessarily.

Your BATNA is not a club you use to beat your business partners; it is your personal limit and safety net to get out of negotiation where there is no middle ground. When you reach that compromise, that is the moment it is time to strike.

Credit, No Credit: The Ongoing Challenge

For most, entrepreneurship comes after working for someone else. It's a reaction to having an idea you can't act on or the frustration of working for someone else. This can be an advantage in more ways than you realise. First, it helps you understand your work style and teaches good work ethics, but it can also help you build the credit you'll need for your first venture.

The fact is, the bank is more interested in loaning money to profitable entities — an employed person is profitable because they are earning a consistent income. The bank can rely on them to pay the interest on their loans. Your new business won't be profitable that way for a few years, making it much less attractive for a loan.

Thankfully, there are ways to leverage the years you spend working for someone else in those initial days of entrepreneurship: borrow every dime you can. If the bank trusts you to extend a personal line of credit, a card with a high limit, anything — you want to have that open credit for overhead costs that you can't avoid, which are necessary to make you profitable.

Why?

Barring a rich uncle coming out of the woodwork, this will likely be the last influx of cash you'll have until your business becomes profitable. It is a calculated risk that you can take to ensure you have a safety net to catch those unexpected bills and not fall into the trap of chasing your tail. Relying on cash from your business is no longer as smart as it once seemed; it is a spell that will keep you spinning in the same place and hamper your growth.

Entrepreneurship is a huge risk that can come with even bigger rewards. Leveraging banking decisions can help you flow from one period of financial challenges to another, but nothing can replace working hard during those moments. You will have to sacrifice comfort during challenging times, but the thread that will carry you through is your vision for your business. It is crucial to have confidence in that vision, as it will empower you to take control into your own hands when you are faced with the inevitable wall of "no."

CHAPTER 9

Venturing into Real Estate

"Ninety percent of all millionaires become so through owning real estate." —Andrew Carnegie[10]

By the mid-1990s, I had a thriving portfolio of businesses and a few rental properties that were making me a little extra money on the side. I had kept my old house in Ayden, North Carolina, and in the late 1980s, purchased a couple of townhomes as rental properties using assumable mortgages.

Until I purchased the warehouse that became Peterson Center, I was working out of a small storefront in downtown Cary as my reupholstery business grew to add fabric sales and a small interior design firm. I was making decent money, and my days of racing to finish a project to have enough money to cover the bills were far behind me — yet I could still feel a piece of the entrepreneurial puzzle was missing.

I was motivated to start the upholstery business because I wanted to strike out on my own; upholstery was a skill I could rely on, and I knew how to sell. I continued to grow because I knew that was the only way to succeed. Once I realized they could be a reliable source of income, I purchased and started managing a few rental properties, but these were all pretty small fry. I focused my efforts on townhomes and single-

---

[10] Source unknown. Commonly attributed to Andrew Carnegie, American industrialist and philanthropist

family rentals, leveraging assumable loans to ensure they were income-generating.

When I built the Peterson Center warehouse, I divided the building into commercial spaces that I could rent out, which meant I was paying for the building using only the rental income. I was doing very well, but I didn't have a vision for how I wanted my business to grow.

The final puzzle piece came to me while on a trip to Wrightsville Beach. My friends and I would walk the docks and admire all the enormous yachts tied up on the water, and I couldn't help but wonder who they belonged to. To give you an idea of what we were seeing, in recent years, the largest "superyacht" to come through Wrightsville had a staff of fifteen people, including two chefs and a masseuse, a wine cellar, and a helipad that could be converted into a basketball court!

That particular boat wasn't around in my day, but the sense of luxury certainly was. My friends and I would occasionally chat with some of the owners in passing as we met them around town, and sure enough — not a single one of them was in the reupholstery business.

I was making a great living. If my ambition or vision for my life ended there, I would be perfectly fine and could likely leave something of a legacy aside for my kids once I was gone. Maybe someday I'd sell my business to someone else and start from scratch if I really wanted a new challenge. I had enough capital and know-how to create a new Peterson Consigning Design and had the income from my rental properties to support it. I was nowhere near destitute, but I was also nowhere near a yacht in Wrightsville Beach. I got to know the yacht owners a little more and discovered that most of them worked in real estate — not only rental properties but also in development and construction! Most of these men were developers or used to be developers; some had unrelated careers but used real estate investment to grow their personal wealth. It made me realize the reupholstery business and my casual rental investments could afford me a nice bass boat, but if I ever wanted a yacht, I was in the wrong business.

All of these yacht owners invested in major real estate projects to protect their wealth and allow it to appreciate over time. Everyone relied on multiple streams of income or investment to help generate their wealth — and none relied on reupholstery. The last piece of the puzzle was finally falling into place. When I returned from that vacation, I redoubled my efforts in real estate investments.

Until then, I used rental income as a casual investment, a little extra cash flow to keep myself flush and my businesses thriving. After that trip I started seriously considering the potential for growth in real estate development and decided to take a more long-term outlook. Rather than buying small properties with immediate cash potential, I decided to refocus on projects that had the potential for development in the long run.

As I had done with the former cookie warehouse, these places could be built upon or redeveloped. I knew I would hold on to Peterson Consigning Design, keeping that steady stream of income and credit, but at the same time, I began to develop my real estate portfolio and put in the work to grow it. Soon after, I got my general contractor's license so I could have a more hands-on approach when it came to new construction.

My biggest mistake would be to purchase undeveloped land and get stuck with it as I waited and hoped for a development bid, so I forced myself to focus on properties that were income-producing right from the start. I wanted to make sure that whatever I invested in could be used as leverage for more credit down the line, and I wanted to continue paying myself so I could grow this new aspect of my business without the panic I felt in my early days.

I discovered that real estate was the boost I needed and the challenge I was craving. The industry is constantly changing, and no day is the same as the next, so I am never bored while managing the nitty gritty parts of my business. I also learned a lot, familiarizing myself with contracting and construction work to capitalize on undeveloped land myself without waiting for someone to do it for me.

My success came after more than a decade of working in another industry, one that is so far removed from real estate that I'm sure many developers, managers, and even bankers who encountered me in the early days thought I was crazy — but that only goes to show that you need to have more confidence in yourself and your vision than anyone else around you.

Real estate has long been considered a stable and lucrative investment option because of its stable market and the ability to diversify your investments while maintaining a consistent income easily. Traditionally speaking, real estate has also been an excellent hedge against inflation. Investment often comes with a few tax benefits, which can significantly improve your return on investment. That being said, it can be challenging to make your mark in the real estate industry, especially early on, but I have a few rules that I always followed that helped when I was entering the real estate market.

Entering Real Estate

For many, investing in real estate seems like it would be a pipe dream, too costly ever to get started, and in some ways, that's true — real estate is lucrative, which means the competition can be fierce, but that doesn't mean It isn't worth taking the time to get into the market. Real estate has the potential for significant returns, can be an opportunity to create passive income, and can become the springboard for other projects or places you've been dreaming of. Success in the industry is hard but not impossible, so long as you follow a few basic rules when you're starting and you're willing to learn from any challenges that come your way.

The first thing to remember is that when you are starting, keep your day job. We covered this briefly in a previous chapter, but you are better off getting financing from your bank with a steady income — don't forget that the bank is also investing in you, and they want to ensure they are getting a good ROI. Anything that interrupts their flow of investment and returns is a risk, and most bankers are not willing to take that risk on an unproven asset. Quitting your employment early will put your safety net at risk and make you lose your borrowing power before you've even started.

This is true for *any* industry, not only real estate. No bank will loan you money until you prove you'll earn it back, so keep your day job until you do.

Lately, there's been a train of thinking from online real estate "gurus," and the like that real estate is a quick ticket to a passive income. I'm here to tell you — it's not. Real estate investment involves constant research and management, a job in and of itself. Allowing a property to waste away because you don't want to put any capital in it will do nothing but put you in a holding pattern and likely lead to you selling at a loss. Maintaining your day job and taking on financing to employ management or create other cash flow gives you time and resources to understand the real challenges in the local market and be able to face them as your business grows.

In the beginning, you'll be doing a lot of extra work, but it is a difficult period that can set you up for success later on. In this initial period, where you're working two jobs, you get to know the real estate market inside and out. To act swiftly and decisively, you need to know your local market — and I mean, you need to know everything.

- How is the area trending?
- Is there a new industry in town, and what is it replacing?
- What kind of road work or improvements are on the way?
- What is the rental history in the area, and how are the schools?

- What is the balance between residential, commercial, and industrial properties?

You learn all of this by putting your ear to the ground and listening. Talk to realtors and brokers, go to town planning and council meetings, become involved in your local organizations, and get to know your area in a way you never did before. Do your research as you build a relationship and credit with your local bank so that you can be well-informed when you take your first step. This will also put you ahead of future investments, as you'll already have a foundation of market research and know where to turn to help you make informed decisions in the future.

In the same vein, this is the time to start building your network and talking to people. As you put feelers out in your market research, let people know you're in the market and looking to expand. While learning, maintain those professional connections and be clear about your goals. Sometimes, you may see an opportunity that would be perfect for your long-term strategy but doesn't fit into your business plan right now; still, be clear that the property is the sort of thing you'd be interested in.

Get to know your local real estate brokers and agents, and make sure they know you — if they can't tell you, they won't think to call when they see something that fits in with your goals. In addition to real estate agents and brokers, make sure to take this time to develop a strong relationship with the bankers in your area. Make sure they know who you are before you go to them for a loan. Share your success, and make yourself predictable in this early stage so it will be much easier to talk to them when needed.

A banker isn't just someone you see when you need a loan; you can also go to them for investment management advice and even ask to talk to them when making deposits — the old-fashioned way. While it is less convenient (and your bank will likely try to make you use their online products), it allows you to become familiar with the banks in your area. Showing your face and building your network this way will integrate you into the local business world faster and more smoothly than investing alone behind a computer screen.

Not only does this give local "gatekeepers" a chance to get to know you and your business goals, but it also acts as another market research method. Don't just get in people's faces; get to know them and their business goals — you never know when or how your paths will cross.

All this preparation isn't for nothing. You want to prepare, research, and develop relationships to act immediately when you see the right opportunity. Remember that a good deal won't sit on the market (sometimes it won't even get to the market, and you'll only see it with the help of a trusted agent), so when you see something that is right, you have to pull the trigger and go for it!

Having a basis of research and relationships allows you to clear the path for the moment you see the right opportunity. Much of the real estate work comes before the deal, long before you own the property — especially when starting. They build on each other and require a lot of work that will spill over into your spare time, but it is a valuable learning experience for the future. A solid foundation will support you as you grow over time and allow you to strike before the concrete is set. As you continue to build and maintain these relationships and stability, you'll be able to diversify and start creating a portfolio of investments.

Diversification: Managing and Maximizing

Initially, staying within your niche is vital; that way, you can maintain better control over your investments without getting overwhelmed. For example, when I was starting, I focused mainly on townhouses because I knew this would be a manageable investment (I could drive over there if there were any problems, and the problems a townhouse might face were familiar to me), and it would generate income almost immediately. Once you have a handle on your real estate portfolio, it becomes time to diversify.

Diversification sounds much more intimidating than it is. Essentially, diversification is a safety net for your investments. By spreading them across a variety of classes, you can manage risk more effectively.

For example, if you diversify your real estate portfolio by including commercial and rental properties, you have something to prop yourself up on if the rental market falters for some reason. Investments respond differently to market conditions, and if you diversify, you can help mitigate overall losses by balancing an underperforming asset with another performing well.

Similarly, having a diverse investment portfolio can cushion the impact of any widespread market downturns. Maintaining assets that traditionally perform well during downturns can offset the losses incurred by riskier assets. An investment portfolio is simply a collection of financial assets you own; it's called a portfolio because of how diverse investments are strategically grouped and managed under a single umbrella — you (or your financial advisor). It spreads your investments across markets to make them more resilient to fluctuations and loss; a diverse portfolio allows you to adapt as economic conditions change by reallocating resources to areas with better growth or resiliency.

To best diversify an investment portfolio, you should be looking beyond a single industry to maximize your ability to bounce back from a downturn in the market. If we're looking at the real estate sector, this might mean investing in residential and commercial properties but also looking at undeveloped land (as a holding, not with the aim of generating immediate cash) and investing in brick-and-mortar businesses.

Beyond that, spreading your investments across different sectors protects your portfolio from industry-specific downturns; having assets in technology, finance, or healthcare can keep the rest of your portfolio from being dragged down if, for example, there was a downturn in the real estate market and you are stuck with properties that are no longer generating cash.

Finally, you can use different investment vehicles to enhance that portfolio push diversification. In addition to a diverse property portfolio, expanding into different industries and markets, you can also look at the various funds you can buy into to secure your assets. Mutual funds, ETFs, and REITs (Real Estate Investment Trusts) are all vehicles to explore when looking for ways to enhance diversification and are more secure than investing in stocks directly. These avenues give you a more steady return and leave the difficult decisions to professionals who are looking at the markets every day; they aren't going to make you rich overnight, but they are a secure place to deposit your money and be sure that it will grow rather than just sitting in a piggy bank.

Diversity in investing is a layered process; there are the small, secure funds that will slowly increase in returns, and on the other side, there are the significant investments that will generate cash more quickly for you. Real estate on its own encompasses many of these layers — you can invest in property directly, expand into different markets by use or location, and invest in REITs and real estate mutual funds to keep your money secure and managed by the best. It preserves long-term wealth by giving you assets that aren't easy to dump in a panic and aren't directly related to the stock market, so you know your investment isn't as volatile as that.

Starting your investment career in real estate is a great decision since it's much more stable than any other industry. Still, it is crucial to remember that real estate should be one part of a broader investment strategy. A successful portfolio is about finding the right balance between risk and return for you and your goals. Using real estate as a launching point, you can create a robust portfolio that weathers the storms of market fluctuations and volatility.

CHAPTER 10

Development Days

"An investment in knowledge pays the best interest." —Benjamin Franklin[11]

After the warehouse and my lightning bolt of inspiration, I started searching for income-generating properties at a somewhat low cost. Townhomes were easy to build and maintain and even easier to rent, so that is where I began. I was still building relationships with bankers and proving myself in the real estate world, which limited my search for investment properties.

I knew I had to dig deep and find undervalued places, similar to the cookie warehouse, to establish my reputation as a capable entrepreneur and developer. The projects that set the stones for the foundation of the bigger projects I tackled later in my career were both residential and commercial: the Broadoaks and Pointview townhomes and the New River Shopping Center. Each taught me valuable lessons about opportunity, taking risks, and the balance of patience and spontaneity.

New River Shopping Center

When I was a kid, my dad often dressed up as Santa Claus and the Easter Bunny at our local mall. The mall wasn't all that close by — it was out in Jacksonville, a short drive from our home in Richlands — and it wasn't much of a mall. The New

---

[11] Source Unknown. Commonly attributed to Benjamin Franklin, inventor, Founding Father of the United States of America.

River Shopping Center boasted your typical mid-market department stores like Sears and Roses, and it had the Ron-Cor where my brother and I used to buy out Boy Scout uniforms, but there was no denying that the NRSC was part of the community.

My dad would often have us act as his assistants during the holidays — to this day, the most embarrassing job I've ever done — as if to remind us that business was as much about community as it was about making money. Years later, when I was just starting as a developer, I came across a classified ad when I saw the old NRSC was up for sale.

I couldn't believe my eyes. By then, many department stores were long gone, and the shopping centre was in disrepair from years of deferred maintenance. It was depressing to see it that way, even if it was the source of some of the most embarrassing years of my life. It was shocking to see it for sale in the classifieds, the same place I hunted for potential deals for sale by owner and priced a little less than their true value.

I called the current owner to ask about the property, and my suspicion was confirmed — the owner had already subdivided the property into a number of smaller parcels, and he was selling two parcels of the New River Shopping Center at a bargain price; take it or leave it, he priced to sell. The parcel he was getting rid of was only half leased. Still, the point at which it would break even was only 25% of its total occupancy — meaning I could keep it running with half the place completely empty and still make money; any improvements I made would only add to my profit margin!

I figured I had to be missing something. I ran the numbers again and again, analyzed the property from every angle I could think of, did all the research I could do, and still came up with the same conclusion: this place was cheap, was already making money, and with a bit of work I could make it incredibly lucrative. I could not figure out why he was selling it. The place wasn't listed with any broker; it was completely off-market.

My banks said the same thing — why would he get rid of it if it's so lucrative? They were convinced there was something wrong that my calculations had been missing and, of course, that meant it took me a while to secure the financing for the sale. Everyone I told had the same reaction, *"If it's such a good deal, why isn't anyone else jumping at it?"* After a long deliberation, I crossed my fingers and took the plunge!

I trusted my instincts, analysis, and calculations; all that remained was to take that final leap. I wrote an offer with as many pathways to get out of it should the property be a house of cards: language to give me an out for any reason, contingencies on inspection, and a long runway to close the deal — you name it, and I bet I put it in that offer. I brought the offer to the owner, Mr. Whichard, an older man who lived in a well-established and stately part of Raleigh, North Carolina.

Whichard answered the door in his bathrobe, his face unshaven, and if I had to be honest, I would say he looked like someone who had rolled in off the street. This unkempt facade hid a serious businessman who knew his business well, even more than I did then. I presented my carefully written offer to him, and he immediately tossed it aside.

"This is what you're going to do," he told me, *"You are going to write me a check for $25,000, non-refundable, and closing in 30 days. I keep the money as of today, and you'll have the two parcels to do with as you'd like."*

When I finally got over my shock, I asked why he was selling the property so cheaply. There had to be some element I was missing; for some reason, he would give up on the property. He told me not to worry that he always left a little money on the table when selling property, but I would still make money and not get hurt with these parcels. Later on, I found out that he was selling for such a low price to generate capital to buy a casino/resort in Reno, Nevada — he was motivated to sell, and I was motivated to buy. At that moment, I knew I would regret it if I threw away this offer, so I wrote him a check and came away with the New River Shopping Center from my youth.

Eventually, Mr. Whichard brought to me another deal — the opportunity to buy a much larger shopping centre in NE North Carolina, a deal that I, unfortunately, couldn't follow through on; however, one of the other owners of the New River Shopping centre called me out of the blue and sold me his parcels of the NRSC. That was the beginning of my gradual acquisition of this odd little mall in the middle of Jacksonville, NC. Currently, there is only one tract of the Shopping Center that I don't own, and it has continued to prove itself. Like the Peterson Center warehouse, I've pulled out my cash and refinanced the land to fund other projects. Yet, this extremely unsexy property keeps going, continuing to make money year after year. And the best part is that I never have to dress up as one of Santa's elves ever again!

Broadoaks and Pointview

In addition to the New River Shopping Centre, I had also developed two townhome complexes; one called Broadoaks — the initial attempt, in which I built and developed 31 townhomes, keeping 15 of them at first to lease myself, but eventually selling all of them; and Pointview, where I kept eight at first, but sold off seven. This was my attempt at creating an income-generating property that would profit from the beginning. That was always my goal in developing real estate; I didn't want to hold onto land and wait for the right moment to develop it. I wanted to make sure the property I had was fulfilling its purpose — a return on investment. Either these townhomes would sell, or they would be rented, though at the time, I preferred selling them.

Unfortunately for Pointview Townhomes and me, the economy took a massive dip in 2007, making it harder to sell since no one was getting financing. Rather than throw in the towel, I pivoted and transformed these into rental properties, single-family units that would help me retain the investment and still generate income during an uncertain time. Since then, I've managed to sell all but one of them, which I keep as a secondary residence in Cary.

The Pointview properties were a massive lesson for me in patience when investing. Just a few years ago, I still owned some of these townhouses that had been rented out rather than sold. I had five remaining, and while they were generating a small, positive return, I knew I wouldn't continue down this road. I was already putting into place my plan for a more considerable development, and single-family long-term rentals were no longer part of that plan — but I did have a lot of equity built up from this development.

I was hoping to use that equity for other opportunities. I wound up selling four of them; with three properties, I could do a 1031 exchange — a tax deferral strategy that allowed me to sell an investment property and reinvest the proceeds into a new property while deferring capital gains taxes. This was perfect for me since I didn't have to lose money to capital gains tax and could use the equity built up in the property towards my new projects.

On the fourth property, the 1031 was completely bungled, and I had to pay the tax liability from my profit. All this doesn't seem like such a bad deal — in the end, I could use the equity stored in the developments (about $400k after the sale) towards another investment, and the tax liability on the last was a small price to pay to have the cash flow pay it forward on the next investment.

However, later on, I realized that had I simply refinanced, I could have pulled about $300k in built-up equity and kept my developments as-is. I already had the management in place, the tenants I had would have continued to pay off my debt, and I would have avoided all of the tax liability — not only that, but I would have benefitted from the continued appreciation of the properties within the next few years!

That would have meant a neutral cash flow — $300k up front, followed by the sustained payments from rental income; plus, when I eventually wanted to sell, I would have seen additional profit and a bigger opportunity when it came to reinvesting in future development projects. In both situations, I made money — but it was clear in retrospect that I would have done better to hold tight to those properties.

In the end, the lesson was invaluable: sometimes, the best move in real estate is to do nothing at all. By holding on to my development and allowing it to appreciate over time, as my tenants paid down the refinanced mortgage, I could have built more equity without the hassle or tax liability of selling. This passive approach can sometimes outperform the more spontaneous strategy, as long as you can see when is the right time to get out.

These selling, buying, and refinancing examples have been the cornerstone of my philosophy since I started in real estate. I've kept properties for long-term appreciation and cash flow, refinancing them when the market was favourable and I could use the cash towards another investment. It is a delicate balance of patience and leverage, knowing the market and trusting yourself while giving yourself room to take risks.

Developing the Underdeveloped

Real growth doesn't happen without calculated risk, and in my experience, the most careful calculations come when considering a diamond in the rough. Every city, town, or neighbourhood has a property that has been passed over because it looks a little shabby on the outside, but with a little bit of care (and money), it could be a fantastic investment.

It might be in a great neighbourhood, or it's more functional on the inside than it seems on the outside; whatever the reason, some potential is waiting to be exploited. Finding gems like these is hard but worth it when you can get in on the ground floor and build it up in a profitable way that compliments the rest of your business and investment portfolio.

Finding properties priced below their market value or underdeveloped can help you generate profit and add your ability to create community and show off your business sense to future investors. Identifying an undervalued property (rather than just another dud) can be tricky.

Finding Hidden Gems

The first step to identifying a truly undervalued property with enough potential to exploit is to conduct thorough market research. Analyzing recent sales data, rental rates, vacancy rates, and other data will give you a clearer picture of what you will take on and how much it will cost you to start generating profits. What you are trying to do with market analysis is draw a picture of the current state of the property and surrounding area so that you can better predict where it is going to go. Without a crystal ball, you need to do this with data that is available to you — the stats from the real estate market.

What else is going on in the neighbourhood? What have other properties been sold for, and what is the difference between those and the undervalued property you are looking at? You want to look for areas with strong growth potential that can rub off on the potential property — areas experiencing economic development or infrastructure improvements or places with high demand for the type of property and limited supply. These are indicators of up-and-coming neighbourhoods or areas with a gap that needs filling.

For instance, you could look at a single-story warehouse with a cold locker once used as a packing plant. This warehouse is in an area redeveloped as a residential neighbourhood, but it was leftover because it would be too expensive to raze and rebuild.

- Could the warehouse be repurposed in some way?
- Would it be a good site for a grocery store, filling the need for basic amenities in a newly developed community?

A gap in the market is not always obvious, but looking around at the neighbourhood and completing some data analysis can give you an idea of what the "gap" is. A little research into planned or proposed developments and municipal restrictions can provide insight into what a property could be. That research is your crystal ball; by looking into the past, you can, in some way, predict the future.

In addition to looking at past performance data, it is crucial to perform a current financial analysis to assess the profitability of an investment opportunity. Consider factors like rental income potential, operating and renovation expenses, property taxes, and the cost of financing — all costs associated with owning the property and how they will affect your bottom line during development. These costs must align with your financial goals and fall into a level of risk you are comfortable with, or you will start to slide into a loss.

A property could look like a wise investment because it only requires cosmetic upgrades or minor repairs; however, the property taxes and restrictions on renovation make it so costly to maintain that it isn't worth the investment.

Here, a thorough comparative market analysis will be your friend; compare the property you are considering with similar ones in the area to understand better why it is undervalued. Investigate what makes this building stand out, for better or worse, to learn why it is priced the way it is.

You should be leveraging your network and online resources to gain a clear picture of what makes the property undervalued. Real estate databases and market reports will help you with the raw data — the legal restrictions on the property, sales history, etc — and your network will give you a more colloquial explanation of the property's conditions.

Asking real estate agents and investors about a property means you'll get insight into someone else's market analysis, and you can compare it with your own goals. You'll learn things the data can't tell you, but a human can; the people in the neighbourhood are just as important as the market data, and only others can tell you about them.

Real estate agents can also give insight into the seller's motivation, which you won't be able to find in a data table. Sellers are motivated for various reasons, and a real estate agent is best positioned to gauge how a seller's and buyer's motivations may align. A seller anxious to dump a property because they are moving or need the equity for another investment won't magically appear in a market report.

Still, you can bet a real estate agent will know exactly who those people are. Making relationships with agents who specialize in undervalued properties can help you find some off-market listings that you would never have found on your own, and they can help with sensitive negotiations that would take twice as long without the insight an agent can provide.

Capitalizing on Undervalued Opportunities

Once you've researched, asked all the right questions, and used your network to help make the right choice, it's time to pounce on that opportunity and start capitalizing on its potential. If you've done your research right, you should know precisely what needs to be done and have the credit required to complete any of those tasks. If your building needs repairs, renovations, or upgrades, it is time to start on them.

An undervalued opportunity is not an excuse to sit on a property and wait for the future to happen to you; it is all about the ability to leverage the potential of a space. Now that the property's value is low, you should take whatever credit you need to renovate, knowing that you will get that back in profit once you either redevelop, rent, or sell the space you're working on. For example, we split the space with the Peterson Center so that multiple businesses could use it simultaneously. Getting started was difficult, but the sooner we could make a space usable, we started renting it out and generating profit from that rent. It is the same quick thinking we've discussed, the instinctual decision-making crucial when working for yourself. Waiting around for someone to give you an answer will leave you hanging for a long time; however, putting a plan into action takes no time. Use all of the data you analyzed and that market research to your advantage — before it changes and the research you did is no longer relevant.

Once the space is modern and usable (either for residential or commercial use), you can start thinking about what you will change. If this is a truly undervalued property, then whoever owned it before wasn't using it to its full potential, or they didn't keep up with market fluctuations, and the building became obsolete. Again, through your research, you should know which was the culprit and can use that information to inform what you're going to change about the building.

If it was once residential, but the neighbourhood has changed, and the demand for rental units isn't there anymore, consider changing it into a commercial space — what would that entail, and what kind of businesses could you get in there?

The alternative would be to flip the space — assuming the market allows for it; if the problem was that the seller was motivated to sell due to financial problems or other short-term gain, a flip could be in your best interests as it could generate enough cash to finance your next project — in this case, you would need to make sure that your renovation costs don't outweigh the value of the property, and that you have a motivated real estate agent to help you sell post-renovation.

No matter what you decide to do with it, an undervalued property can be a massive asset to your real estate portfolio, helping you generate more profit than buying something at market value and muscling growth from there. The real estate market is dynamic, so your strategies for finding new projects must be as current as possible. Taking time to search for undervalued properties deliberately might be the key to gaining that fresh perspective.

Searching for hidden gems helps you stay informed about market trends, neighbourhoods, and local bylaws that could affect your other properties. It's imperative to keep learning and refining your investment approach and to challenge yourself to take on projects that aren't "perfect" at first sight. Implementing some of these strategies helps you maintain a disciplined approach to analysis and investment, which will, in turn, help tune your business acumen towards a good opportunity for you and your portfolio.

Keep in mind that real estate markets are highly localized, and projects like this can help you develop a deep understanding of the dynamics in your target areas. With careful research, strategic planning, a solid network, and the willingness to act fast, you can unlock the hidden value of your real estate market and help drive the growth of your business.

Successful real estate development is an art form that requires you to be an analytical thinker and creative strategist; you have to understand your numbers, do constant research, and stay flexible in your outlook and decision-making. Your properties are more than just buildings; they are financial instruments with the potential to generate wealth and create opportunities for future investments — the key element is to recognize how to leverage your properties to benefit your larger goals. On the one hand, you have to trust your instincts; on the other, your instincts might lead you astray and teach you lessons you didn't want to learn.

Numbers tell a story, and in real estate, they are your most reliable narrator. Relying on your gut instinct is fine once you've tuned that gut instinct to steer you the right way. Until then, numbers will be your best friend. The most successful developers know that every decision is backed by solid financial data that informs the risks you are willing to take. This means calculating all different kinds of key metrics, most notably:

- Return on Investment (ROI): How much profit you stand to make relative to your investment. If this is a rental property, you will calculate the (reasonable) rental income against your mortgage and maintenance costs and how long it will take to start generating a pure profit.

- Capitalization Rate: The property's net operating income as a percentage of its purchase price.
- Break-even Analysis: How long will rental (or other) income take to cover your investment and expenses?

These calculations help you paint a clear picture of whether a project is financially viable. Trust in your numbers comes from doing research and being disciplined enough to listen to that research. When a deal is too good to be true, it is — but if you've run your numbers, and they align with your research, perhaps it's just a good deal. This is why you must build trust and confidence in yourself because you ultimately make the investment decisions. This personal trust will also help you avoid making emotional decisions that contradict the due diligence you've already done. If the numbers don't add up, no amount of personal hope will make them. On the other hand, if you add up the numbers to a fantastic deal that falls into the undervalued category we discussed previously, trusting that you did the work could lead you to a great deal that others have ignored.

In real estate, timing matters as much (if not more) than execution. Waiting strategically can lead to much better outcomes, whether by holding onto a property as it appreciates in value or seizing on an undervalued opportunity before someone else does. While selling properties can provide immediate capital for reinvestment and give you the flexibility to pivot or start new projects, sometimes patience offers more long-term benefits, eventually allowing you to do the same.

Rental properties, in particular, can be powerful wealth-building tools. They generate consistent income that can cover overhead costs (like your mortgage or maintenance costs) while producing additional profit. These properties usually appreciate over time, meaning that even an unglamorous property can become valuable. As the property's value increases, you get the opportunity to refinance and create a new cycle of cash flow, leveraging your initial investment against future opportunities.

It is all about balance: action for the times opportunities arise and patience when there's a chance for long-term growth. These decisions should be held up against your market analysis and forecast of local trends: you should always know what is happening around you and the broader world, as that can affect every aspect of your property. The advice here is just for hypothetical situations, but it isn't the law. It's important to throw out the rule book and start writing your own when necessary.

CHAPTER 11

Overcoming Naysayers

*"Many an optimist has become rich by buying out
a pessimist." —Robert G. Allen[12]*

There's a theme in my career that is subtle enough that if I didn't talk about it, you might not notice. I have dealt with many people from all walks of life throughout my career, whether it was developing property or working in upholstery, and many of them have had opinions about my abilities that I disagreed with — they've been naysayers. In every aspect of business and any industry I've come up against, I've had to face someone who felt they were a better judge of my abilities than I was.

It's an extremely frustrating and infuriating position to be in, but one that is inevitable as an entrepreneur. Whether it is banks or people, you'll meet naysayers who either think they know better than you or want to offer advice, and it is difficult to determine whether that is constructive or condescending.

I've talked a lot about banks turning me down and having to find alternatives, but people will also turn me down. I've made deals that took ten minutes and others that took months to come to an amicable conclusion. The first house I ever bought was an exercise in working with naysayers. I was

---

[12] Source unknown. Commonly attributed to Robert G. Allen, American author and motivational speaker.

21 years old, had barely started my career, and was buying with no money down, so convincing the owner to sell it to me and finding financing was the first of many delicate negotiations I've had to do.

I read a book called *"No Money Down"* by the businessman Robert G. Allen, which guided me in finding hidden opportunities and creative negotiation strategies for buying properties with little to no upfront cash. The book is practically a bible for those who need to think outside the box when finding investment properties. His main idea was to leverage other people's money ("OPM") and find creative negotiation points to persuade the seller to let you buy the property.

Allen talks about focusing on sellers who are motivated to sell quickly or properties that are undervalued and using creative financing and negotiation techniques — using "sweat equity" in exchange for reduced down payments, taking over existing mortgages, or even bartering with trade to find ways to get a seller to trust in your ability to buy.

Allen's guide is helpful in many ways, but the most important lesson I took was to be confident to face those who thought they knew better than me. It showed me that I could persuade someone to change their mind with research and creativity. Since then, I've learned that many people who like to dole out advice don't always have experience with what you're asking — your banker won't always know, nor will your accountant, spouse, or best friend. If you listen to anyone, it should be someone who is too busy to dole out advice and will instead give you a little constructive criticism before sending you on your way. That criticism — usually in the form of telling you what was wrong and what you should be paying attention to instead — is where you can glean a bit of wisdom.

Many naysayers will doubt your abilities; they will also doubt your vision for a property or business. Your confidence in yourself and your work will be your saving grace. I've had experiences that have taken me over two months, with circular negotiations that led nowhere, but I had the confidence to stay the course. I have learned over the years when to leverage patience or a little arm-twisting but the through line has always been to turn back to my personal vision and business plan.

Even in the first few properties I bought, while the bank and sellers didn't have confidence in me, I did, and those experiences taught me that the only opinion that truly matters is your own. While it may take time to develop your business acumen and instinct, yours is the only one that will keep you on the right path. Whether it is a banker who is hesitant to lend money because he thinks you're in the wrong industry or a seller who wants to make your life difficult because they don't have the creativity to see your vision, these naysayers will crop up in every part of your life. You can't avoid them, but you can learn a few things that will help their words roll off your back a little more easily.

How to Cast Aside Naysayers

In your business, as in life, you'll be fielding many opinions about what you should or shouldn't be doing. Somehow, the voices that are always loudest are the naysayers, those who focus on the negatives and always manage to find the flaws in your plans. Every once in a while, constructive criticism may come through that can help illuminate a problem you missed, but for the most part, many of these naysayers are more focused on themselves than you.

Regarding bankers, they are taking care of their bottom line; real estate agents and brokers are thinking of how your decisions will affect their client base or portfolio. In business, just as in life, you'll have to find a way to drown out those voices if you hope to succeed. Overcoming naysayers requires you to have a plan of action and an abundance of confidence to sort the constructive criticism from the unhelpful pessimism. Knowing the difference between the two takes time, but with a few key strategies, you will quickly turn back to your instincts when making that final decision.

Constructive Criticism vs Pessimism

Naysayers come in many forms — they might be friends, family members, colleagues, or bankers — typically, their criticism stems from a place of concern or fear of the unknown; sometimes, it's from their unfulfilled ambitions; either way, it's important to maintain trust in yourself and your business instincts. That way, you can listen to the motivation behind their negativity and use it to fuel your decision-making, and figure out what is constructive criticism and what is plain pessimism.

So, what is the difference between constructive criticism and pessimism? Constructive criticism is a form of specific, actionable, and intentional feedback. It focuses on results rather than personal beliefs and is usually followed up with clear guidance on the next step. Most importantly — constructive criticism is invited; if you estimate a property valuation and ask for a second opinion, you might receive some feedback you didn't want to hear.

If the feedback is something like, *"I think your valuation is a bit high, based on my own sales data for the area. Maybe we should compare our notes and see if we can determine a new valuation based on our combined data,"* that can be considered healthy constructive criticism. Your second opinion sees something wrong with what you presented and is looking to help you fix that. Their feedback aims to help you re-evaluate the property and motivate you to continue your project rather than shutting you down.

In contrast, pessimism, or criticism for the sake of it, lacks specificity or actionable advice. It focuses on what went wrong and does not offer a path for improvement. This is often vague and can target you as an individual rather than evaluating your business decision. This is the type of criticism you can — and should — feel free to ignore. If someone tells you "you don't know what you're doing," without explaining how they came to that conclusion or giving you actionable advice on improving, then you can be assured that their opinion is not worth your worry.

The best way to keep the criticism of a naysayer at bay is to turn them into allies. Those you interact with on a business level can become part of your network if you listen to their (constructive) concerns and follow up on those with merit. To use the same example as before, if you make a property valuation and present it to a real estate broker for a second opinion, taking their constructive criticism into account could lead to a collaboration.

Those willing to offer constructive criticism likely have something valuable to say and can offer a valuable opinion — or even a significant lead on a property — in the future. It's better to listen to their concerns and follow them with a grain of salt, considering the helpful advice and getting rid of the rest. Follow up by sharing your success, not to show off but to demonstrate where you accepted their advice and where your instincts served you well. This professional back and forth can help build your relationship and get that other professional on your side, which could benefit you in the future.

Ultimately, you don't know how a critic can help you down the line, and you don't know who will be a successful business partner until you have the patience to listen to them. While I will always say that you should trust your instincts over those of a naysayer, I also believe it is better to have friends in your network rather than enemies; the only naysayers who matter are those you can convert into supporters.

Opportunity for Growth — Finding Inspiration in Naysayers

Not everyone can be converted from a critic to an ally; there will always be those who persist in pessimistic or ignorant critiques and prefer to find holes in every plan or solution you present to them for reasons you'll never understand. That's the key detail to remember here — you will never understand.

Why bother wasting your time trying to dissect their psyche?

Instead, draw your inspiration another way. These pessimists won't provide constructive criticism, so you must turn inward if you don't want to sink to their level. Use their negative feedback as a catalyst for your improvement; stay focused on your goals and supportive network to drown out the noise from naysayers who aren't genuinely interested in your success.

Harnessing that negativity and using it as fuel to drive your personal goals is the best way to fight back against naysayers uninterested in your success. Using the same example as before, say you take a property valuation to a second opinion, whose only response is that you're doing it wrong and don't know what you're doing. Rather than sink to their level or crawl into a hole of self-doubt, use your skills to prove that you know what you're doing.

In this case, you could go back to your research to establish your valuation is correct or fill in any gaps that might lead to an inaccurate valuation. Re-analyze recent market trends and look for growth or other positive markers to counter the pessimistic naysayers who say your outlook is overly optimistic. Using this negativity to fuel your positivity will not only make some of your naysayers eat their words, but it can also help your personal development by forcing you to go back over your work and find new opportunities you might have passed over. There will always be obstacles in your work, both personal and practical; drawing inspiration from naysayers will help you practice overcoming these obstacles. It's best to view challenges like these un-constructive critics as opportunities for growth and to strengthen your vision for your business.

To avoid backsliding into self-doubt, reinforce your business instincts by reviewing your business plans and goals. Evaluate your success/failure benchmarks and current business goals to remind yourself what is vital in your business plan. Doing so might have you readjust, but you might need that commitment to get those naysayers off your back.

For example, when working on the warehouse in Cary, which eventually became Peterson Center, I could not get the financing needed to pay for a contractor to clear the building. I re-evaluated, knowing that this warehouse was crucial to my plan and its success was key to my own, and decided to complete the work myself. Doing so helped me create a plan to divide the warehouse into multiple units, increasing my profit. It also reduced the overhead I'd have to pay to a contractor and alleviated some of the reliance I had on getting credit from a bank.

I could focus on paying necessary tradesmen while doing much of the work myself. In the end, re-evaluating my original plan (to get funding from a bank and pay a contractor) benefitted me more than fighting with the bank — I reduced spending by doing much of the work myself, leaving a higher margin for profit once the building was completed. Rather than sink into self-doubt, the rejection motivated me to work harder, resulting in a better outcome because I stayed true to my vision and plan.

Everyone's a critic — at some point, even you have been someone else's naysayer! There is a significant difference between someone who is critical but encouraging of your success and someone who is a critic for the sake of it. There are times when these two might sound the same, when the voices of the naysayers start to blend, and you can't tell the difference between what is constructive and what is pessimistic. In those moments, it is crucial that you stay true to your instincts and goals because that is what will help you stay the course.

Criticism is part of personal growth, as is hearing negativity, and as you grow with your business, you'll learn how to listen to naysayers. Your instincts and expertise will always be more important than someone who wants to dismiss that, but you can use their pessimism as inspiration or a catalyst for improvement. You can also learn from constructive criticism and turn some naysayers into important nodes in your business network, leveraging your success to make a good impression on them.

The best way to succeed is to learn from your mistakes and grow. Ignore the naysayers, cast off the pessimism, and focus on your business goals and benchmarks — in the end, that is more important than humbling yourself to someone else's negativity.

CHAPTER 12

Family in Business

"Like branches on a tree, we all grow in different directions yet our roots remain as one."
—Suzy Kassem[13]

My entrepreneurial career started with a small upholstery business run out of a spare room. Still, it has blossomed into multiple properties and businesses where I can collaborate and mentor my children and watch them grow alongside the developments we work on. I didn't set out to have my kids follow in my footsteps; though it may seem that way, my goal was only for my kids to have more opportunities than I had. When I worked for my dad, I never got paid — there was simply no money to pay me with — instead, I got a second job at night to have some money. I didn't want my kids to feel my despair, but I didn't want just to hand them everything on a silver platter. I wanted to be able to provide assistance, mentor, or train them in whatever path they chose.

Working with my family has come in so many different stages, from having my son Mike practically demolish a building and clean out greasy pipes alongside me to partnering with my daughter Ashley after she proved herself at Peterson Consigning Designs. Ashley had always had trouble in school and, for a long time, thought she had a learning disability. When she started working for me, she wasn't the greatest

---

[13] *Rise Up and Salute the Sun: The Writings of Suzy Kassem.* 2010.

employee, and she didn't have her heart in the business, and it showed.

Eventually, we lost our manager, and I promoted Ashley after she delivered an impassioned plea... because we didn't have anyone else. Once she became the manager of PCD, she came into her own, educating herself and improving the store. It was then that she learned there was no learning disability but that a structured school environment wasn't for her. She studied business independently and has used her unique learning style to her advantage ever since, growing Peterson Consigning Designs into a successful store with record-setting numbers year over year.

I have more memories than could fill these pages of my children as they were growing up; narrowing them down is practically impossible. My son Connor, who was six years old, set up a mobile shop (their wagon) full of beanie babies for sale. They sat there every day for two weeks without making a single sale, and then in the third week, I found out they raised their prices!

Why?

Connor calmly explained that the new "book" came out, so the toys were more valuable, and the price needed to reflect that! When I ask my kids now, they seem to remember more of the hard work I had them do ("hard labour," according to them) and that I never let them have it easy when it came to work. They had a job to do, and if they had a problem, I was there telling them to figure it out — whether it was getting to work on time or how to mow grass at the trailer park I owned.

It was harsh at the time, probably more harsh than is acceptable nowadays, but my kids reflect that it forced them to figure things out independently and learn how to problem-solve. These days, I enjoy a close relationship with all of them, both at work and outside the home.

Our relationship is close and colloquial. I can go to them with any concern and vice-versa; ultimately, that is the relationship I hoped to have with them. I never forced my children to stay in the family business; a few of them have split off and followed their path. My son Chris, for example, still works with me — he manages a property we developed together and the adjoining restaurant — and is the only one of my children to go to a formal college, where he graduated with honours from the MBA program at East Carolina University. I never felt the need to graduate from college; I don't think it's necessary, but Chris used the time to his advantage and has been successful. It worked for him but not for me, and ultimately, I am here to support him rather than hold him back.

My family has become a vital aspect of success in all parts of the business. My eldest, Mike, has been there since the beginning, doing a demo with me on the Cary warehouse that became Peterson Center, and even started his own moving company while working for me. Ashely is now a partner in Peterson Consigning Design, and my other son Chris is a partner in our restaurant, Surf City Line, and in the Island Inn Motel. Connor is also involved in our properties at the beach, managing our vacation properties, Turtle Shell Properties. The only one of my brood who isn't in the family business is Cary, though he purchased Mike's moving company and has forged his path in the business world.

I sometimes struck gold with a group of kids who all found a way to use their strengths and have an entrepreneurial streak. Still, I often wonder if I could encourage that with my approach to parenting and involving them in the business. I maintained boundaries with all of them, making sure they knew if they were working for me, they had to be working. I also made sure they all knew I was around as a mentor and a guide, no matter their path, even if it diverged from my own.

No matter what — even after I separated from their mothers (which may have happened a few times) — I made sure they knew I wasn't going anywhere as a father figure. I have always been a leader when I needed to; whether I realized it or not, that was the key element missing when I started working for my father. He was wrapped up in a failing business and couldn't be the mentor or leader that the business needed.

When I struck out on my own, he was among the first to tell me it was a hopeless path. Without intending to, I became a different leader from my dad by staying true to myself and always keeping a balance between my children and our work.

Family Teams, and How to Keep Them

Working with family has benefitted me both personally and professionally. I can mentor my children, see their success firsthand, and spend plenty of quality time with them. We've already talked about strategies to avoid conflict when merging family with business, so in this chapter, I'll focus on strategies to integrate family and the unique challenges therein. Family businesses form the backbone of local economies worldwide and go back hundreds of years. Take a look around your town or city and count how many "& Sons" businesses you see — it's usually quite common to integrate your network into your business, in part because the labour is cheap to start with but also because many people want to pass the legacy of their business onto those closest to them.

We'll explore some strategies for successfully incorporating family into your business structure and highlight the benefits that family partnerships may bring. This integration is more than just employing your relatives; it's about creating a connection between family bonds and business acumen. When done well, it can give your business a competitive advantage, bring fresh new perspectives, and empower you and your family.

Benefits of Family Partnerships

Family partnerships offer unique advantages that can significantly contribute to success and longevity in the business world. Leveraging the strength of family bonds can create resilient and highly successful enterprises, so long as you find productive strategies for making that partnership. What might begin as a summer job can blossom into a life-long business partner, with a few key benefits: a shared vision and similar values for your company, a greater sense of trust and commitment at work, and having a sounding board for flexible decision-making.

Trust in your business partners is crucial when making big decisions and following your instincts. This means searching for a business partner you can confidently trust and share your vision of the future for your business — a difficult task when so many entrepreneurs have such strong personalities.

When working with family, you can benefit from the fact that your vision and success will benefit you and those around you, and you are working with someone you inherently trust. From observing them all our lives, family members usually deeply understand each other's strengths and weaknesses. That familiarity gives you trust that can take years to develop in non-family partnerships.

Family members are also more likely to stand by each other as they weather the storms of a downturn rather than jumping ship. This deep bond can create the sense that your business is a legacy to be preserved and passed down rather than a temporary stop on the way to greener pastures. It creates an environment where everyone is gunning for the business to succeed and excited about what that means — a communal commitment rather than an individual one.

The communal trust extends to knowing each other's limits and instincts, which means your business can benefit from a more flexible and faster decision-making process. If you are working with your child and they inherently know your negotiation style, they can make decisions without you that will still be true to your business style. Suddenly, you have an environment where you can eliminate the long and tedious back-and-forth of decision-making, one that is inevitable in situations where everyone you work with is a stranger.

The close-knit nature of family relationships can facilitate more open and honest communication since family members are often more comfortable expressing their opinions or proposing new and innovative ideas. This can benefit your business immensely since, assuming your family is just as knowledgeable as you are, you have a built-in second opinion that you already trust.

Of course, as we discussed before, this open family relationship comes with its difficulties and baggage; openness can become combative, and that free flow of communication requires added patience to be beneficial — but the benefits of having your family on your side when it comes to business generally outweigh the difficulties that can arise when working so closely together.

Structures and Strategies for Integrating Family

Right now, I'll say there is no right way to integrate your family into your business. Some decide to start them out young, having their kids tag along or do "chores" to help them familiarize them with the business; others decide that their children or partners should get a little "real world" experience before diving into the family business. The way I did things may not apply to how you run your business, but that is very fair!

However, there is a wrong way to integrate family. Forcing your kids or partner to work for you because they are the last resort, the only option for profit, or your ego will only breed resentment and likely result in a failed business venture. Muscling a partnership like this can lead to you ignoring their natural strengths in favour of your idea of who these people are or even outright ignoring their faults and weaknesses.

Before integrating your family into your business, keep in mind that you will become a team that works together towards the same common goal. If one of you is resistant or resentful of that, it will hold the whole business back.

The first step in integrating family into business operations is establishing a robust governance structure within your business. That is a very corporate way of saying you need to explicitly define the roles and responsibilities of each family member and where they stand in the hierarchy of your business to avoid overlaps, confusion, and potential conflicts.

This also means you need to objectively evaluate their skills to make sure you are keeping a sense of professionalism within your organization. A well-organized structure includes outlining your objectives and job description, defining performance metrics, and establishing clear reporting lines based on what is already in place. This ensures your family members understand their expectations and where they stand within your business structure, and hopefully, outlining your expectations for them will prevent unnecessary conflicts between them and your employees who aren't part of your family. The last thing you want is for your family members to come running to you whenever they have a problem, which can foster negative feelings between them and their peers.

This likely sounds very impersonal, maybe even overly corporate, for a family business. After all, this structure or way of working has been going on for hundreds of years! It sounds formal because, on paper, it is. When you are face to face with your family, it won't feel quite as explicit, partly because of your relationship, but the idea of having a formal governance structure is that you have a defined boundary for where your personal relationship ends and your professional one begins.

If you are planning for a long future with your family business partner, you should also take into consideration a formal shareholder agreement between you to make sure everyone is aligned on key business — and financial — matters. By creating a document and setting these boundaries, you can reduce the potential for disastrous misunderstandings and build a stable foundation for your partnership.

A huge part of why you want to create this type of structure is to help establish clear conflict resolution protocols for working with your family. Conflict will inevitably arise at work — if you can't avoid it at home, why would you be able to at the office?

Having a structure in place can prevent the most common pitfall of working closely with those you love — having personal and professional lines crossed in an argument. It might be a formal discussion, a family meeting, or something more informal, but you have to take a moment to establish a separation between work and family time.

We've discussed this before, so I'd encourage you to take another look at Chapter 4, but having these lines blurred can lead to misunderstandings and strained relationships in the long run. It's normal to get into arguments with your family, and it's healthy to be able to resolve them; by establishing these boundaries and conflict resolution structures, you are thinking ahead to avoid making the inevitable any worse than it has to be.

Looking Outward

Family businesses can benefit from one unrelated personal relationship — engaging external experts can help address sensitive challenges and provide unbiased guidance when working with family. Professional advisors can help provide a second opinion or navigate complex issues where you might struggle to let go of your bias. Your family is your team, but taking in consultants or getting a second opinion can — as I've said before — expand your network beyond your personal circle. Bringing in new opinions can reinvigorate your ideas and inspire family members to think outside the box.

As a leader, you want to mentor your partners and set an example of work ethic; as an entrepreneur, making connections and expanding your network is a major part of business growth. In this way, encouraging your family to look outside the company for new business leads or second opinions helps them understand that success in business doesn't occur in a vacuum and can help illuminate solutions and opportunities they wouldn't have seen by themselves.

Adaptability has always been the key to success for entrepreneurs and small businesses; family businesses must remain open to innovation even though the structure is a more "traditional" way of working. In a way, integrating family can help your business immensely, especially when you're talking about uniting different generations.

Younger family members bring new ideas to the table to help you stay competitive — they can also bring new connections, networks, and ways of doing business. Keeping a focus outward while allowing your family to benefit from your mentorship maintains that same growth mindset we've talked about before. You are a leader, but you now benefit from having a junior who isn't afraid to challenge you. Integrating family into business is as much a learning opportunity for you as it is for them.

Integrating family into your business requires thoughtful planning, a deliberate commitment to professionalism, and a willingness to embrace change. Those boundaries might break down or change over time, but in the beginning, it's important to create some structure to establish a solid and stable foundation. By adhering to a few awkward practices, family businesses can grow and thrive while maintaining harmony among family members. Ultimately, you know what your family can offer; you likely spotted the potential, or else you wouldn't be looking for ways to integrate them into your business!

CHAPTER 13

The Sunset Project

*"Patience, persistence, and perspiration make an
unbeatable combination for success."*
—Napoleon Hill[14]

There is one project that I hesitate to call my Magnum Opus, though others might disagree. It started as a piece of undervalued, underdeveloped property: a trailer park that I purchased and managed for a number of years, hiring my kids to do maintenance and landscaping. As time passed and frustrations with the tenants began to build, I started to look at expanding, gradually persuading the land owners around me to sell and talking to the town about turning it into something better.

I took on development partners and investors for the first time. I faced new challenges as I took a leap forward in my career as a developer: planning and building a whole new community from scratch rather than renovating industrial spaces or building single-family townhomes. The project at Sunset Lake, also known as Peterson Station, has taken over ten years to complete and countless headaches to even get started. It is a shining example of where determination and a forward-thinking attitude can get you and that adaptability and openness to change can take you very far.

Peterson Station is the largest development I've been involved with so far in my career, with 316 luxury apartments

---

[14] Napoleon Hill, *Think and Grow Rich* (1937)

and 47,000ft of retail space. By now, it's also the most valuable investment I've made, with an estimated valuation of $150 million at completion — but this was never my master plan. I purchased a trailer park of about 7.5 acres years ago because I would instantly be making an income off it.

There were already residents on that land; it was up to me to collect rent and maintain the grounds (work I assigned to my sons, Chris and Connor, who still enjoy griping about getting dropped off at Sunset Trailer Park in the thigh-high grass with nothing but a couple of push mowers and water coolers). Still, all that was a lot of work. This property was different from the townhomes that I had already been renting. The residents were mostly low-income, and it was not for the faint of heart; drugs and crime were rampant, and for a while, I was in a constant revolving door between Sunset Park and the courthouse as we sued for back rent or to try and evict the more dangerous tenants.

I remember receiving a complaint from a tenant that needed to be repaired inside one of the trailers. I went down there with my eldest son, Mike, in tow. He was about 17 at the time and reminded me a lot of myself at that age -- enterprising, hard-working, and with an eye to the future. We walked into the trailer, and the condition of the place blew my mind!

Roaches were crawling all over the place, and trash was strewn about; it was clear the place wasn't being well taken care of. Mike and I made our way to the back of the trailer, where we found a leaking sink and a floor desperately needing repair. I knew what had to be done, but I also knew my boundaries as the property owner and manager -- I took a long look at the debris around me and walked right out. Mike, dutiful as ever, asked how we would start fixing it, and I told him to forget about it; I wasn't going to go in there, and neither was he. He was surprised; he thought we needed to fix it; that was when I told him I would never ask him to do anything I wasn't prepared to do myself -- an abiding philosophy that Mike has carried over into his management style.

I told those tenants that until they cleaned up the interior, we wouldn't be able to go back inside. A few months later, they moved out, and the structure was so damaged it could only be torn down. This sort of thing wasn't uncommon -- I remember another incident where I sent my sons to collect rent, and one of the tenants tried to sell them drugs!

These incidents motivated me to change the use of the property, and I started looking into rezoning and possibly annexing it. As each tenant vacated their mobile home, I decided not to replace them and instead have the structures torn down. The development would take some time, and at that point, I wasn't sure what to do with it; fortunately, I had enough income from other businesses and properties to make up for the loss as I made a plan for what to do with Sunset Trailer Park. It took many years to move forward, but my big break finally came when Holly Springs annexed the trailer park into their town.

Holly Springs annexing the trailer park into their town from the county was *enormous* as this meant I could tap into their water and sewage systems. With the trailer park in the county, I could only have access to the community well and individual septic systems, severely limiting what I could build on the land. It wasn't sexy, but it was a start! In about 2007, after the area was annexed, I went to the town. I had the property rezoned to "neighborhood business", meaning I could construct a small strip-mall on the 7.5 acres -- but before I could even get started, the economy took a major hit with The Great Recession of 2008, and everything came to a screeching halt!

I tried to replace the trailers that had been removed to make up for the fact that there was now no opportunity to build, but the town wouldn't allow it -- we had successfully rezoned it as a business area, not a trailer park, so there was no going back. The property just sat there for the next few years, barely making any money, as I (impatiently) waited for the next opportunity.

It took another seven years or so to get the ball rolling again. By then, I'd had many, *many* conversations with colleagues over the best use of the property -- did we try again to build a strip center, imitating what we had done at Peterson Center or the New River Shopping Center?

- Should I go back to the town and re-zoning *again*?
- Should I just cut my losses and sell the lot?

Finally, my architect and good friend, Chet Vanfossen, realized that, while a 7.5 acre project would work, it would be even better if I could assemble a larger tract of land to do something even bigger, like a mixed-use project. That was when the idea for Peterson Station arose in earnest: a project that combined luxury living spaces with businesses, capitalizing on commercial and residential rental income. At that point, I hired a couple of real estate brokers to try and buy out my surrounding neighbours to put my plan in motion. Everyone failed to convince the owners to sell; instead, they tried to tell me to stick to my 7.5 acres -- either develop it or sell and move on. Stubborn as always, I decided to approach the neighbours myself.

At first, I tried to buy out one of my neighbours who had 1.5 acres, with a plan to construct a much smaller project -- but he held out. In fact, he ended up holding out until I had purchased seven of the eight surrounding lots! After his rejection, I pivoted and approached each of the other owners.

After several months, I managed to get every piece of property under contract -- including the initial holdout. I went to them personally, so they got to know me as an entrepreneur and explained my vision for the area. What had once started as a trailer park could be transformed into something more, something that was safer and offered more opportunity and value for the town. Once I had the parcel of nine units -- a collective 20.5 acres of land -- I started the development process. One that is certainly not for the faint of heart.

First, I had to get the property entitled, meaning I needed to have my new property rezoned and approved for its intended use. That was no easy feat, as it meant countless meetings with town officials, council members, planning board members, the Mayor of Holly Springs, and even the neighbouring communities -- all to drum up support and explain how my project would benefit the community at large.

A development like this one requires a *lot* of cooperation from the town and a lot of persuasion on my part, as the town has its vision and ideas for what that 20.5 acres could be! Without support from the town, I would be stuck in the same place I was before -- sitting on acre upon acre of land without the zoning permission to do anything with it. To get this project properly zoned, I went before the town council on three separate occasions, and the length of time was such that the council members had *changed* three times since my first appearance!

The entitlement process was a long and highly detailed process with changing site plans, architectural plans, engineering plans -- everything you could think of, and a little more to persuade those against it to cross to our side. By then, I was starting to run a little low on money, so I brought on a few investors for the first time in my career. The first was the same friend who convinced me to take on such a huge project in the first place, Chet VanFossen. He was a former town council member and was instrumental in helping me navigate the town officials and get my project approved.

The civil engineer on the project also became an investor, and I also turned to my friends and family to help raise additional funds to get us across the finish line! I felt a tremendous boost of confidence and pride when I saw my community rally around me as they invested in my idea despite the fact that the project wasn't even close to starting! A development project like Peterson Station takes a long time, and it is easy for fellow investors or even yourself as an entrepreneur to give up and move on.

I remember early on in this whole process, after I had assembled the nine properties, but before I presented Holly Springs with my plans, a developer friend of mine said to me: "Jeff, you've done extremely well assembling all this [land]... I can make two calls right now, and you'll walk away with *millions*." A wiser man might have listened, considering his offer as he weighed it against his years of frustration. Instead, I asked him:

"What would I do with millions?"

"You could get yourself another project!" He countered. I laughed and asked, *"Why I would do that when I already had a project?"* I was never going to pocket the money and sit on it, twiddling my thumbs at home, so what was the point in giving up and not seeing Peterson Station through to the very end?

Maybe if I had known how long and grueling this process would be, my answer would have been different, but at the time, all I could think was -- what else would I do?

The only obvious solution when faced with that question is to keep going.

With Peterson Station, I learned that perseverance, determination, and sheer stubbornness can help you overcome any hurdle you encounter. At this point, the project to build Peterson Station has taken over ten years. While not unheard of for a project of this size, it's hard to believe it's been so long. There's one reason I've kept going through challenges with sellers and other developers, municipal agreements and entitlements, financing issues, and a predicament with the local wetlands: I don't quit.

Once I take on a project, I am always determined to see it through to the very end. That being said, if I had known at the start how long it would take and how many obstacles I would face, I most likely would never have started the project! I at least, would have made a more strict plan of action to plan for the many obstacles and financial challenges that cropped up. A long-term plan would have made Peterson Station more predictable; while that might have been daunting, it would also create a path to profitability and completion that I didn't get as I made decisions on the way.

Patience and Planning in Long-Term Projects

In my life as an entrepreneur, I've learned that patience and long-term planning are essential ingredients for success. In real estate, in particular, projects can sometimes stretch for years or even decades — as with the Peterson Station project. Not only that, but they can sometimes snowball into other projects, builds connected to your original development, or expansion opportunities; in this industry, patience and planning are the foundation on which empires are built. These crucial attributes can make or break your ventures in the complex world of entrepreneurship.

The Planning Paradox

The fast-paced world today makes patience seem like a quaint and outdated notion; however, in real estate development, it can be a strategic advantage. The ability to wait for the right opportunity, to hold onto the property until market conditions are favourable, or even to navigate municipal processes successfully can be the difference between success and failure when it comes to getting ahead in real estate.

Long-term planning is like playing a real-world game of chess — the best way to work is to think further than your next move. You're strategizing for a few moves ahead, balancing your plan with the ability to think on your feet. Many obstacles in real estate development are predictable if you research, such as connecting with municipalities through town hall meetings, planning commission meetings, zoning hearings, and general assemblies.

Attending these meetings will help you get to know the market and the place you live and can contribute immensely to your long-term plan; for example, zoning laws and regulatory changes happen all the time, and being aware of what your city has planned or what they are aiming towards will help you navigate costly changes in your planning or redirections in construction. Not only that but attending municipal meetings can also help you build crucial relationships with local officials and community leaders, relationships that might smooth the path of future projects through mutual trust and understanding.

Real estate landscapes are littered with cautionary tales of short-term thinking; developers and investors who rush into projects without due diligence or those who overlook long-term issues in favour of quick turnarounds and profits often face overwhelming challenges that force them to redirect or cast their projects aside. Impatience can lead to overlooking critical issues, missing opportunities for expansion, financial strain, and, most critically, damage your reputation as a business owner. Developing patience and a long-term perspective is hard, especially since you want to simultaneously develop the other side of that — the ability to jump on opportunities as they appear. Business strategy is an odd balancing act — how do you cultivate patience while working towards success in this lifetime rather than the next?

Patience and planning skills, like many others, are passive skills that you need to work on to succeed in your entrepreneurial endeavours. The skills aren't different from many of the topics we've discussed in this book — we've already talked about making sure to continuously educate yourself and the importance of building a diverse portfolio, even the importance of developing strong relationships with your community — even strategies that contribute to a growth mindset! All of these elements come back into play when talking about cultivating patience.

The more you understand market trends, economic cycles, and urban planning, the more comfortable you'll be with long-term strategies. Having a deep understanding of these concepts helps you to distinguish the forest from the trees as you create your business plan — if you step back for a moment and see market trends on a wider scale, you start to see more than the local opportunities in front of you. You will also start seeing patterns of development, gentrification, or even loss in the market that won't come up if you're analyzing the market for short-term profitability.

Developing comprehensive plans based on your research that can adapt to changing conditions over time allows you to bridge the worlds between short and long-term thinking. Take the plan with the trailer park, for example; I started by searching for a property that would be income-producing from the start.

Once I realized it wasn't a good long-term plan, I began to change course passively, but I wasn't sure of where to navigate. I had enough knowledge of the market to know that the land was being underused, that based on its location, it could be redeveloped into something that would benefit the community and be successful in the long run; however, with a long-term strategy in place, I would have been more capable of navigating the municipal, financial, and logistical challenges that cropped up during the development.

Flexibility is still crucial when creating these long-term plans. In part, it is because flexibility makes patience a little easier — waiting around is a little less stressful when you have a backup plan or other projects to focus on — but also because it creates pathways to pivot when the unexpected comes up. A significant factor affecting our budget and timeline on the Peterson Station project was the 2020 COVID Pandemic, a global epidemic that no one could have predicted. It put a halt on construction projects and made everyone rethink the value of their investments — including myself.

By this time, I had another project on the go — more on that later — and plans for luxury apartments at Peterson Station, alongside retail and commercial properties. This crisis affected our bottom line and the financial resources available for development over ten years in the making, and a little short-term flexibility allowed the project to keep going rather than stall completely.

Rewards of Patience and Planning

Those who can master the art of patience and planning in real estate are set to reap some fantastic rewards. Taking the time to plan and properly execute your developments often results in higher quality builds, renovations, and deeper relationships than those focusing on the short-term route. It also offers greater profitability and sustained returns;

developing relationships with community members often leads to securing better terms in future deals and loans and even finding more high-value properties from community leaders who have come to trust you. Long-term thinking fosters stronger relationships with your stakeholders, from investors and bankers to community leaders and tenants.

Ultimately, the longest-term project you want to work on is your business. While you'll likely have many long-term projects, especially as you invest more in real estate, none will last as long as your business will. Everything in this chapter — flexibility, patience, and research — can relate to your long-term business goals and success just as much as the individual projects you'll work on. Cultivating patience within your business pursuits helps you translate that patience into individual projects and also means you won't burn out early with only a few short-term successes under your belt.

CHAPTER 14

Beachin' It

The world is your oyster. It's up to you to find the pearls." —Chris Gardner[15]

By 2019, the Sunset Lake project was still stalled. Financing and finalization got in the way, and while my plans were at a standstill, I decided to turn my attention to a new venue -- the beach. I had been spending more and more of my time down in Surf City, North Carolina -- a few short miles from Richlands, where I grew up -- and during that time, I started to see all the new opportunities cropping up in the area. I already had a small investment there: The Tipsy Turtle, a large oceanfront property I had built several years earlier. I had been using a local rental company to manage leasing the place to vacationers and was pretty hands-off in all things beach-related -- except when it came to relaxation.

As the delays continued at Peterson Station, I grew increasingly antsy at the beach. I couldn't relax and found myself craving an outlet, some way to be productive with all the time I had as I waited for Peterson Station to start construction; Peterson Properties and Peterson Consigning Design were in trusted hands, with Mike and Ashley each running their respective show, and there wasn't a reason for me to meddle.

I had a fantastic office manager, Angela, who was the glue responsible for keeping all my business ventures in sync. It

---

[15] Chris Gardner. *In Pursuit of Happyness*. Amistad, 2006.

was the perfect moment to dive into a new project, and Surf City was the perfect fit. Instead of resigning to sipping piña coladas on the beach, I started Turtle Shell Properties.

We started with the building that would later become Surf City Line restaurant, which needed major renovations before it could become anything. I encouraged my son, Chris, the general manager of Peterson Builders, to come down to the beach and run the renovation projects and expansion with me. Once he was on board, we could really get going with Surf City Line and the apartments behind it, the Turtle Shell Bungalows — and before we could do very much, the pandemic hit, and everything shut down. I remember we were knee-deep in both construction projects but couldn't decide which to prioritize with the strange circumstances of the COVID pandemic.

My son Chris and I decided it would be best to finish the apartments first since people always needed a place to live and restaurants were completely closed down with no clear date to reopen. We slowed down work on the Surf City line and re-distributed our resources to get the bungalows going, and I'm glad we did! Once the apartments opened, they were monumentally successful from the first day, and I think they are the most profitable venture I've ever done, all things considered — especially since the cost of remodeling the Bungalows exceeded their purchase price!

Most people see the finished product and all the success that came from it, and they think we're just lucky to have been able to accomplish it all. Of course, what they don't see are the sweat and tears, the planning headaches, the constant back-and-forth, and the anxiety-inducing fear of financial loss. As I've always said — luck is a matter of opportunity and preparedness.

Chris and I were prepared to let go of Surf City Line to complete one of our projects, and since we weren't dividing the labour, we had the opportunity to finish it sooner than otherwise. The pandemic may have taken a wrench in our master plan, but in my life, I've learned repeatedly that things don't always go as planned, and you need to take a hard look at your priorities and what is more critical down the line.

Once the pandemic panic was over, we were finally able to complete and open Surf City Line, which added to the success of the bungalow — and came with its own set of unexpected challenges (turns out, running a restaurant is nothing like running a grill line — much harder to figure it out on the fly), but the success was evident, and it opened the doors to more opportunities in the area.

A realtor friend, Sandy Wise, called me about a quadplex in the area that was about to go on the market and asked if I was interested. I immediately agreed, banking on the snowball effect of the success with Surf City Line and the Turtle Shell Bungalows. Many of the places I was offered were pretty dilapidated, and this place was no exception, but I knew the market well and was confident I could turn it around. The property was right across the street from another one of my properties, and I already loved the location, so I agreed to the full price and said it would close in 30 days with no inspection necessary. Sandy was hesitant for a moment, but I was sure, so I told her to go ahead and make the deal. I thought that was it; I'd found my next project by the beach — or so I had thought.

An hour later, Sandy called me back and told me there was a problem. The seller received six other offers, each considerably higher than mine. The seller felt a little guilty for agreeing with me but was obviously tempted by the other, higher offers, so Sandy told me to hold off on doing anything, to wait and see if the seller would agree to honour our deal. I didn't want to lose it, so I told Sandy to pass along a better offer: I'll agree to whatever price he wants to sell to secure our deal.

Meanwhile, I hopped in my car, blank check in hand, to ensure I could get pen on paper as soon as possible. The seller increased his price by $25,000, and by the end of the day, I was the one who secured the property. While the seller received twelve other offers, all much better than my original one, I was willing to complete the sale on the same day — which, ultimately, is much better than an offer, with its many contingencies and holding patterns.

It was thanks to Sandy, in the end, that I was able to pull off such a quick buy — if Sandy hadn't been there to assure the seller I was a trusted and qualified buyer, it's more than likely the seller would have gone with one of the many better offers, without a second thought to mine. The relationship I had created with the realtor secured the property, along with my willingness to jump at the opportunity — preparedness, opportunity, and I was the lucky buyer for that quadplex. Once again, my son Chris and I spent about as much money renovating the place as I had purchasing it, but we've flipped it around to become Turtle Shell Hideaway, another piece in our short-term rental puzzle.

At this point, Chris and I were well-oiled machines. I found new (old) properties while Chris ran the construction. Not long after finding Turtle Shell Hideaway, I found an old motel for sale for a few years. It was still being used, but it was in very poor shape from all of the deferred maintenance, and I knew it could be a gem if someone — anyone — could get their hands on it and restore it to its former glory.

I had already passed up an opportunity to buy the old motel and let a friend of mine know about it since he was also considering moving down to the beach. His offer fell apart when his partners decided there was too much work to do for the property to be of any value, but based on my experience, I knew the property was a diamond in the rough, and there was a path to turn it around; renovating was only the first step, the next would be to change its designation from a motel to short-term rentals, leased individually.

After my friend's offer fell through, the property sat empty for another six months with no one interested, so I decided to try and purchase it myself. I reached out to Sandy Wise, the same realtor who helped me with the Hideaway, who contacted the seller for me. I could have gone to them directly, but I wanted to repay Sandy for her help with the other properties, and I knew she would likely have a better rapport with the motel owner than I since she knew the area fairly well. In talking with the seller, Sandy learned she was open to selling at a lower price and that the last deal had fallen through mainly because the previous buyer had inadvertently insulted her about the property's condition.

Thankfully, Sandy and I knew better; it was clear that the seller of the motel had an emotional connection to the property, and part of the disrepair was due to financial strain, not because she didn't care. The motel was another extensive renovation, but once again proved a fruitful investment. It's been rebranded as Turtle Shell Key West, a collection of 6 small studios and two complete apartments, striking the perfect balance between short-term rentals and that motel nostalgia.

We didn't stop there; we've continued expanding to include other Turtle Shell properties (Turtle Shell Palace, Turtle View, Turtle Nest, and The Waterway) and another motel renovation, the Island Inn Motel, all of which have continued to be successful thanks to the thriving beach tourism in the area. Surf City Line, the restaurant, has rolled into other commercial properties, like the 10th Street Bar and Carolina Decor, a retail and consignment shop -- and this isn't the end for us! There are plenty more projects along the way.

It all goes to show that in times of frustration; it pays to look for another way to renew your inspiration. Since taking over the management of the Tipsy Turtle, we've assembled an all-new team to manage the developments that grew from that opportunity -- Turtle Shell Properties. I've also roped in another of my children, Connor, to manage the vacation rentals under the Turtle Shell umbrella while allowing my other son, Chris, to grow as the general manager of Peterson Builders and a partner in Surf City Line restaurant!

To create this network of entrepreneurship, it is essential to bring on those you can trust and rely on to work to your professional standard. My children have repeatedly risen to the occasion; by now, their skills surpass my own! Seeing their progress gives me the confidence to keep going. The beach was probably my opportunity to lay down my pen and stop signing these deals; instead, it introduced me to a whole new market, new colleagues and partners, and a new way of doing business! All because I was open to the opportunity and didn't allow frustration to get in my way.

Beachside Connections

Turtle Shell Properties came seemingly out of nowhere; a home purchased as a vacation rental plus an opportunity borne out of frustration isn't necessarily a common formula for a successful investment, but it turned out to be a learning experience that snowballed into a profitable venture. Once again, opportunity and preparedness created ideal circumstances but were not without challenges. Turning a casual investment into a more serious venture is not easy. It requires planning and development in a beach community, which is unique, unlike investing in a city property.

Crafting Coastal Communities

Moving into a beach community requires a keen understanding of these areas' challenges and opportunities. Beachfront properties have an undeniable allure: the promise of stunning views, premium rental income, the potential for appreciation, and consistent turnover make them attractive investments for those looking to relax between projects. At the same time, it can be easy to look at beachfront properties with rose-colored glasses and ignore the risks involved with diving into these investments. Beachfront properties come with their tenant woes and environmental considerations, and they aren't always as easy as beach life might make them seem.

Oceanfront locations always command premium prices — it's easy to market a room with a view to people who want a relaxing vacation. It's harder to manage the risks involved with those premium locations. As a developer, it is crucial to factor in environmental risks and seasonal fluctuations to better predict your profit and plan for success. Not only that, but beachfront communities often have more complex regulations and zoning laws to protect the area's natural beauty and — especially with the growing concern over climate change — to protect their fragile ecosystems.

Also, beachfront communities are subject to more intense weather events than their inland counterparts, meaning special consideration has to go into building materials and insurance costs. When investing in the beach, it's essential to be prepared for a potentially lengthy and costly process; it is sometimes better to find a property and renovate rather than develop a plot of land from scratch.

Before committing to the project, make sure you are investing time and resources in comprehensive, specific research, including localized market analysis, environmental impact studies, and all the relevant local regulations governing this coastal development. When the time comes to expand or gain the confidence to start on a new build, you'll have the background to complete your project without any regulatory hiccups.

In this day and age, some future-proofing for your properties can also be an excellent investment; incorporating sustainable and resilient design elements can help your projects — whether they are new builds or renovations — get approval and enhance their long-term value. Resilient construction uses materials and strategic design to help withstand coastal weather conditions, including storm-proofing and flood resistance; eco-friendly features and building materials can also appeal to new markets, like environmentally conscious buyers or renters who hope to minimize their environmental impact while vacationing.

Contributing to a beach community doesn't have to be isolated to your individual property. You can enhance the market value of your property and those around you by taking a proactive approach to the infrastructure around your property. Working with local authorities to enhance roads around your property can improve accessibility and potentially increase property values for yourself and those around you. In remote locations where certain utilities, like internet connectivity, are harder to access, connecting with the municipality might be the easiest way to increase profitability and revenue — and enhance your relationships in the local community. Beachside towns tend to be places that are tight-knit, with a combination of local residents and seasonal residents who have been visiting for years.

Cultivating connections within the community will help you gain support for your projects and keep you from being isolated or shut out entirely from decisions that will affect your investments and developments in the future. Balancing your business interests with those of the community can be particularly challenging in coastal towns, as they are typically sensitive to elements that would not be present in other developments.

Beach towns are more likely to ask questions about preservation or expansion and how your development will coexist with the current businesses in town. The best thing to do is practice proactive compliance — design your project around the town rather than coming in with a bulldozer and an idea. In all communities, careful consideration and negotiation are key to a smooth development process; in a beachfront community, this is even more important to make your planned investment successful.

Going Pro: Turning a Casual Investment into a Profitable Venture

Transforming a casual investment into something more requires a little strategy, but it mostly takes a willingness to adapt how you do business. A casual property is usually more hands-off; it might be a property where you've hired a management company to do all the work, so you don't know it as well as something you manage yourself. Deciding to take a more hands-on approach means taking over an investment with its structure and making delicate changes to increase long-term profitability. This is likely an investment that already has its management in place, and swooping in requires you to adapt to the existing structure to make sure it transitions to a place of success rather than blowing up the business as it stands.

First, you need to pinpoint where your interests align with market opportunities surrounding the property you want to convert.

- What skills, hobbies, or expertise do you possess that will elevate the property and turn it into a more profitable venture than it already is?

- Is the problem down to management, or has it been marketed poorly?
- Is this a matter of changing its use?

Once you're able to identify how you want to change, you can go ahead and start planning for it. For example, turning a building from a vacation rental to a restaurant requires knowing the market (what restaurants are already available, what has been popular in the past?

A Michelin-star, tapas-style restaurant likely won't do well in place of a beach-side taco spot), and also the capacities of your space (Is the building able to support conversion with a dining room and full kitchen?). Your research into the market, competition, and regulation will help you tailor your investment to meet the area's specific needs, increasing your chances of turning it into a major success.

For the most part, you need to treat the transition as a new business entirely. The difference between a casual and more serious investment is the time spent on one versus the other; because you haven't spent as much time developing this business, it's best to start from scratch, using some of the techniques we've outlined previously. In this case, your success/failure benchmarks will be a boost, as you can define what this business will be in the future. Crafting a new business plan is also helpful, in part to plan the transition from outside management to in-house and ensure this transition goes smoothly.

While it is tempting to scale quickly, it is best to focus on sustainable growth so you can better absorb and implement feedback during your transition. Listening is crucial as you explore what needs to change for your business to be profitable; that means listening to the community and your employees or fellow investors, who may have valuable insight into how your casual investment can improve. Remember that when taking over a casual investment, other people know the day-to-day workings of the business better than you, and those stakeholders will probably have ideas of how the business can grow organically. Staying open to new ideas and being willing to pivot when necessary can be a significant competitive advantage and will make you a proactive manager during a heated time.

Conclusion

*"Do not follow where the path may lead. Go
instead where there is no path and leave a trail."
—Ralph Waldo Emerson[16]*

As we near the final pages of our journey, it's worth pausing to reflect on how far we've come from my earliest days learning lessons of resilience while camping with my brother Gary and about what hard work means in the tobacco fields of North Carolina to set up my own business with no overhead, shifting focus later in life, and navigating the complexities of a significant real estate development covering over twenty acres!

This memoir isn't just about recounting my life and reminiscing about my glory days. I hope it is also a testament to resilience, hard work, and the relentless pursuit of something more. Each chapter represents a stepping stone towards building an entrepreneurial career and shaping the mindset needed for lasting success.

Life rarely takes us down a straightforward path. There are twists, turns, setbacks, and unexpected triumphs. When you read this book, you may get the impression that every project and every deal was perfect — I analyzed the deal, put pen to paper, and the rest was history! Sure, I had some trouble with the bank, or renovations took too long, and construction ran

---

[16] Source Unknown. Attributed to Ralph Waldo Emerson, American philosopher and poet.

over budget. Still, ultimately, every project I came across turned out to be a huge win, teaching me a few valuable lessons along the way. Before you close this book, I want to emphasize that there have been many missed opportunities for every win. For every deal that went perfectly, another fell to pieces before my eyes. For all my hits, there were still some misses. I didn't have time to mention them all, but I am tempted to talk about one since the beach properties are fresh on my mind.

There was a property at the southern tip of the island many years ago that slipped through my fingers. I know I've said it enough times by now, but I will say it again: luck is opportunity meets preparedness. I encountered the opportunity this time but wasn't prepared at all. The listing included four lots, a building, and some dockage. It was listed at a fair price, and I knew the area was expensive, so it seemed to be a good deal; however, when I looked at the property, I found out the four lots included the building.

I felt misled and unhappy with the listing since it became far less valuable, having been split up this way. I walked away, no harm, no foul. It wasn't until six months later that it finally hit me. I was looking at the property all wrong! I was so focused on the land, the lots, and the building that I missed a glaring opportunity: the dockage. The docs were old and rundown, but in that area, CAMA (the Coastal Area Management Act) regulations complicated the construction of new docks. Renovating an existing dock would have brought immense value to an already highly sought-after property! Of course, by the time I realized it, the property had long since been sold. My hubris — focusing on the land and being annoyed at its misrepresentation — lost me a property because I wasn't thinking about the bigger picture.

This story is only one of many I could tell you and is merely an example of how life takes twists and turns, always teaching you lessons along the way. Through this book, I have tried to illustrate the outcomes, mindset, and principles that have guided me through the uncertainty of entrepreneurship. This memoir isn't about one man's success story. It is about embracing perseverance, adaptability, and continuous learning.

What's Next

So, I can hear you ask, what is the next twist in the path?

What does life have in store for me now?

As it often goes, my plans will probably change a dozen times over the next year. I'll suffer disappointments with some, and others will be more successful than I imagined, but regardless of the outcome, I'm thrilled to be this busy.

Peterson Station is full in on the commercial leasing for 47,000ft of retail! One of the spaces will be a 2nd location of the salon concept that originated at New River Shopping Center, Evolution Salon Studios. The second location will consist of 30 individual suites, available to rent by beauty professionals — owning the real estate and charging myself rent has been a win-win situation. The rest of the retail spaces are currently being actively leased or pre-leased with restaurants, bottle shops, coffee shops, and possibly a satellite healthcare facility!

At the beach in Surf City, we are simultaneously working on several projects: 60 apartment units for rental; an even larger beachfront house for short-term rentals to be added to the Turtle Shell Property offerings; a twelve-unit ocean view property to be combined with the Island Inn Motel; an expansion of our commercial properties that will allow for more retail; and, of course, actively searching for smaller properties to purchase and convert to vacation rentals.

Finally, in Cary, we are exploring the possibilities around renovating Peterson Center, as the area has exploded and is now brimming with potential. With a fair amount of certainty, I can say that there's a strong possibility that many of these projects will be expanded, added to, adjusted, and who knows what else! With the ability to adapt quickly on the fly and with my team at hand, I know we will be successful.

Key Takeaways and Advice

Each chapter in this book has taught you something new. Whether it is how to integrate family into business without tearing each other's hair out or how to achieve a growth mindset that will help you expand your entrepreneurial pursuits, this memoir has allowed me to pass along some of the lessons I've learned throughout my long career. At the end of the day, you can read all the books you want, but the only way to succeed is to get out and get started. That's the best advice I can give you. The rest is scattered throughout the book, but I want to collect key insights here as a final impression.

- Don't quit your day job when starting the transition into real estate. Most people think real estate investing will quickly lead to a passive income, but nothing can be further from the truth. The reality is there is nothing passive about real estate; once you purchase a property, you might have to renovate or develop it, and even after that, you have to continue managing it! If you quit your employment too early, you'll risk more than is worth and lose your borrowing power.

- You have to know your market. To act swiftly and decisively, you must know the market like the back of your hand, which means everything.

  - How is the area trending?
  - Is there any new industry on the way?
  - the rental history of the area?
  - Are there any schools around?

- You learn all this information by putting your ear to the ground and listening. Talk to as many realtors and brokers as possible, and take in everything they say. After that, go to all the town planning and council meetings and get involved in local civic organizations. Getting to know the area is crucial, and putting yourself out there and getting to know your network will make things easier in the long run.

- Get to know your local bankers. That's paramount to continued success. Make sure they know who you are long before you ask them for a loan. Your relationship with your banker affects how much credit they are willing to risk with you later on; a banker who knows you are predictable will be easier than someone who doesn't know you or your business. They need to know they can trust you, and the only way to build trust is to have them get to know you over time — not only when you're sitting across from them asking for a loan.

- Rely on your network. Let people know you're in the market and looking to learn. Once again, you can do this networking by getting involved in local community organizations and networks. The more you get to know the realtors, brokers, and developers around you, the less you'll have to search for properties that fit your bill. Eventually, you'll find those properties are presented to you by the same people you developed relationships with in the beginning.

- When the right opportunity strikes, act immediately. A good deal won't sit on the market — it may not even get there in the first place! So be prepared with everything I mentioned: market research, a willing banker, and a robust network, and pull the trigger! Again, the only way to succeed is to get started.

As we close, I encourage you to reflect on this advice and consider your journey. Whether you're just starting and looking for guidance on how to get going, in the middle of your career and thinking about expanding or maybe redefining your entrepreneurial goals entirely, remember that the power to create your future is in your hands. The lessons I've shared are yours to carry forward. Let this journey serve as a reminder that with some hard work, a vision of the future, and a willingness to embrace the unknown, you can carve out a path that is all your own.

www.ingramcontent.com/pod-product-compliance
Lightning Source LLC
Chambersburg PA
CBHW061757120626
46550CB00005B/2026